Multi-Ethnic Literature

- ☐ Afro-American Authors
- ☐ American Indian Authors
- ☐ Asian-American Authors
- ■ Mexican-American Authors

Mexican-

HOUGHTON
MIFFLIN
COMPANY

BOSTON
New York
Atlanta
Geneva, Illinois
Dallas
Palo Alto

American Authors

Américo Paredes

Raymund Paredes

Library of Congress Catalog Card Number: 75–160038

ISBN: 0-395-12740-8

ACKNOWLEDGMENTS

Grateful acknowledgment is made to authors, publishers, and agents for their permission to reprint the following selections.

"Among My People," by Jovita González, from *Tone the Bell Easy*, by J. Frank Dobie, published by the Texas Folklore Society, 1932. Reprinted by permission of the publisher.

"The Bending of a Twig," by Alfredo Otero y Herrera. Copyright *Arizona Quarterly*, Vol. XXV, No. 1 (Spring, 1969). Reprinted by permission of the author and publisher.

"Cecilia Rosas," by Amado Muro. First appeared in *New Mexico Quarterly*, Vol. XXXIV, No. 4 (Winter, 1964). Copyright, the University of New Mexico Press. Reprinted by permission of the author.

"Corrido de Jacinto Treviño," collected and translated by Américo Paredes. Appeared in *Buying the Wind*, edited by Richard Dorson, University of Chicago Press, 1964. Reprinted by permission of the publisher and author.

"El Hoyo" and "Señor Garza," by Mario Suarez. Copyright *Arizona Quarterly*, Vol. III, No. 2 (Summer, 1947). Reprinted by permission of the author and publisher.

"The Engagement," "The Street of the Cañon," and "The Street of the Three Crosses," from *Mexican Village*, by Josephina Niggli, University of North Carolina Press, Chapel Hill, 1945. Reprinted by permission of the publisher.

"Guitarreros," by Américo Paredes. Published in the *Southwest Review*, Vol. 49 (Autumn, 1964). Reprinted by permission of the publisher.

"The Immigrant Experience," by Richard Olivas. Appeared in Octavio Romano's "The Historical and Intellectual Presence of Mexican Americans," *El Grito*, Vol. II, No. 2 (Winter, 1969). Reprinted by permission of the author and Quinto Sol Publications.

"The Legend of Gregorio Cortez," from *With His Pistol in His Hand*, by Américo Paredes. Copyright 1958, University of Texas Press, Austin. Reprinted by permission of the publisher.

"Maestria," by Mario Suarez. Copyright *Arizona Quarterly*, Vol. IV, No. 4 (Winter, 1948). Reprinted by permission of the author and publisher.

"Maistro," by Arnulfo D. Trejo. First appeared in, and copyrighted by, *Arizona Quarterly*, Vol. XVI, No. 4 (Winter, 1960). Reprinted by permission of the author and publisher.

"Pedro," from *Crazy Gypsy*, by Luís Omar Salinas. Origenes Publications, Fresno State College, Fresno, California, 1970.

"The Purchase," by Nick C. Vaca. First appeared in *El Espejo*, copyright 1969. Reprinted by permission of the author and Quinto Sol Publications.

"Rancho Buena Vista," by Fermina Guerra, from *Texian Stomping Ground*, by J. Frank Dobie. Published by the Texas Folklore Society, 1931. Reprinted by permission of the publisher.

"Sunday Costs Five Pesos," by Josephina Niggli. From *Mexican Folk Plays*, edited by F. H. Koch, University of North Carolina Press, 1938. Reprinted by permission of the publisher.

"To an Old Woman," by Rafael Jesús González. First appeared in *New Mexico Quarterly*, Vol. XXXI, No. 4 (Winter, 1961–1962). Copyright, the University of New Mexico Press. Reprinted by permission of the author.

PHOTO CREDITS

Page viii (Américo Paredes), University of Texas, photo by Frank Armstrong; p. 52, the University of North Carolina Press; p. 93, photo by John Myers, collection of Dr. and Mrs. Martin I. Durst.

Contents

Introduction 1

Corrido de Jacinto Treviño 5

Jovita González 8

Among My People 8

Fermina Guerra 17

Rancho Buena Vista 17

Américo Paredes 27

Dichos 27

The Legend of Gregorio Cortez 35

Guitarreros 51

Josephina Niggli 52

The Street of the Three Crosses 53

The Engagement 61

The Street of the Cañon 68

Sunday Costs Five Pesos 76

Rafael Jesús González 93

To an Old Woman 93

Mario Suarez 95
El Hoyo 95
Señor Garza 99
Maestria 105

Luís Omar Salinas 111
Pedro 111

Amado Muro 113
Cecilia Rosas 113

Arnulfo D. Trejo 127
Maistro 127

Alfredo Otero y Herrera 132
The Bending of a Twig 132

Nick C. Vaca 141
The Purchase 141

Richard Olivas 149
The Immigrant Experience 150

Spanish Words and Phrases 151

About the Authors

AMÉRICO PAREDES

Américo Paredes is Professor of English and Professor of Anthropology at the University of Texas at Austin, where he is the director of the Center for Mexican-American Studies. He has taught graduate and undergraduate courses in American and Latin-American folklore. He was graduated from the University of Texas, where he also earned his master's and doctor's degrees in English and Spanish. Currently, Dr. Paredes is editor of the *Journal of American Folklore* and a member of the editorial board of *Folklore Américas.* He is the author of short stories and poems. Two of his major published works are *With His Pistol in His Hand* (1958) and *Folktales of Mexico* (1970).

RAYMUND PAREDES

An assistant professor of English at the University of California at Los Angeles, Raymund Paredes received his doctorate in American Civilization from the University of Texas at Austin, where he was an instructor in American Studies and editor of *El Chisme,* the newsletter of the Center for Mexican-American Studies. He has participated in the Stanford University Chicano Studies Institute and has taught in Los Angeles and El Paso public schools. Dr. Paredes is a member of the Modern Language Association, the American Studies Association, and the Organization of American Historians. His research interests lie in American ethnic literature and American social history.

Introduction

People like to record their experiences; Mexican-Americans have been no exception. They have had much to write about. Their lives have sometimes been stormy and often tragic, but always vital and intriguing. It is hardly surprising that Mexican-Americans have literary talents, for they are heirs to the European civilization of Spain and the Indian civilizations of Mexico, both of which produced great poets and storytellers. Furthermore, they have also been in contact with the history and the literature of the United States, for Mexican-Americans have played a key role in the cultural development of the American Southwest.

Although their homes are in the United States, much of the literature of Mexican-Americans has been written in their first language, Spanish. Only during the last fifty years or so have they written widely in English. This book deals almost wholly with what Mexican-Americans have written in the English language; that is, it surveys only their literature of the past half century. Mexican-Americans have gone through considerable change during this period, and so has their literature. You will note some clear differences between the earlier selections and the later ones in the book.

The earlier selections offer examples of what we call "folklore." Folklore, which may be defined as "the unofficial heritage of a people," is usually passed from one person to another by word of mouth. It includes such things as legends, jokes, songs, stories of adventure, and proverbs. To the Mexican-American his folklore is especially important because he belongs to a bilingual minority: he speaks two languages. His "official" heritage, usually learned in school, is expressed in English, and he shares it with all other Americans. But his folklore is for the most part in Spanish, and

The Aztlán Territory

it belongs to him alone. The ballad "Corrido de Jacinto Treviño" and the *dichos* (proverbs and other sayings) presented here have been translated from Spanish into English. The Spanish versions of the *dichos* have been included to show how these examples of folklore look in their original language.

Folklore is important in another way: it is the very core of a people's literature, the foundation on which many great literary works are built. Shakespeare, for example, frequently used English folklore in his plays. The great Spanish writer Cervantes used many proverbs and folktales in his novel *Don Quixote*. In the United States Herman Melville, Nathaniel Hawthorne, Mark Twain, and John Steinbeck are some of the many writers who have used folklore in their fiction. Josephina Niggli is a Mexican-American writer who knows her folklore well.

Folklore is significant in still another way. History books are very often the biographies of great men—the Washingtons, the Lincolns, the Miguel Hidalgos and Emiliano Zapatas—but little may be said of what ordinary persons thought and felt. Folklore is the history of the people, not the presidents and generals in Washington, D.C., and Mexico City, but the *campesinos* (country people) in South Texas and Chihuahua.

Besides traditional folklore, this book includes stories, nonfiction, poems, and a play. Some of these selections were written before World War II, when most Mexican-Americans lived in rural areas; it is only natural, therefore, that literature of that period describes life in small villages, haciendas, and farms. Many stories of that time are basically "romantic"—that is, they are adventurous and emotional, displaying an optimistic faith in mankind.

The literature of the period after World War II is quite different. The stories are usually set in cities and focus on aspects of urban life. They deal with such problems as education, drugs, juvenile delinquency, and the loss of Mexican culture. Much less optimism is expressed: Amado Muro, for example, in "Cecilia Rosas" describes a Mexican-American girl's lack of pride in her heritage. Some of the writers are clearly angry. Nick Vaca accuses a cruel and tactless Anglo world of mistreating the Chicano, while Richard Olivas bitterly questions the relevance of the American educational system. To many students such problems will seem very familiar.

While the various Mexican-American authors may express different viewpoints and attitudes, a number of them are telling their own versions of the Chicano experience. And this is very important, because many Anglo writers have been less than fair and compassionate in their treatment of Mexican-American character, culture, and history. This book is an attempt to swing the scales back toward a proper balance. Stephen Crane, in his western stories, saw the Mexican-American as cowardly and stupid; but in this volume Josephina Niggli sees the Mexican as daring and resourceful. While John Steinbeck, in *Tortilla Flat*, pictured the Mexican-American as totally incapable of handling his financial affairs, Mario Suarez here presents him as a competent businessman. In this book the Texas Rangers do not always slaughter Mexicans like so many ducks on a pond; the Mexicans, on the contrary, win a few battles themselves.

After all, history can be a matter of interpretation. In this book a *barrio* is not necessarily a squalid, filthy slum, but a vital, lively neighborhood where people lead a warm, dignified existence, though they may not be reposing in luxury. This is not to say that Mexican-American writers idealize their own people without any awareness of their human faults, for this would be to distort their life styles in another direction. Mexican-American writers do not claim that their people are perfect. They do claim for them a basic equality in virtue (and vice) with all other people.

One last point. Surely a great lesson Mexican-American writers can teach all Americans is the fundamental absurdity of national boundaries. You will notice that the selections which follow are set not only in the southwestern United States but in northern Mexico as well. For the Mexican-American writer—indeed, for the Mexican-American people as a whole—all this vast area is one land. The Mexican-American recognizes the Rio Grande not as a boundary but as a great life-giving artery running through his homeland. The Aztecs had a name for that vast territory—Aztlán. This book is by and about the people of Aztlán.

Corridos are Mexican folk ballads. Often those that originated on the Mexican-American border tell of skirmishes with the Texas Rangers. The Rangers, employed by Texas as law-enforcement agents, do not appear in the corridos *as heroic figures, but rather as enforcers of Anglo oppression. These* corridos *narrate the courage of Mexicans who stood up for their rights against the Anglos.*

Jacinto Treviño lived in Cameron County, Texas. In 1910 he killed an Anglo-American who had killed Treviño's brother. As a result, he had a gunfight with Texas Rangers and sheriffs' deputies who tried to kill or capture him. Though several of his opponents died, Treviño escaped unscratched into Mexico. This corrido *is still sung on the Texas-Mexican border, and a college in southern Texas is named El Colegio Jacinto Treviño, attesting to the lasting popularity of this Mexican-American folk hero.*

The following version of the ballad was collected and translated into English by Américo Paredes and first appeared in Buying the Wind, *a book of American folklore.*

Corrido de Jacinto Treviño

It happened once in McAllen,
In San Benito, that's twice;
Now it has happened in Brownsville,
And we have seen something nice.

In that saloon known as Baker's
The bullets started to fly;
Bottles would jump into pieces
Wherever you set your eye.

In that saloon known as Baker's
They scatter and they run;
No one is left but Jacinto
With rifle and pistol-gun.

"Come on, you cowardly Rangers;
No baby is up agin you.
You wanted to meet your daddy?
I am Jacinto Treviño!

"Come on, you treacherous Rangers;
Come get a taste of my lead.
And did you think it was ham
Between two slices of bread?"[1]

The sheriff was an American,
But he was shouting aloud,
"You are a brave man, Jacinto;
You make the Mexicans proud."

Then said Jacinto Treviño,
Laughing so hard that it hurt,
"Why don't you just kiss my elbow
And fold the cuffs of my shirt!"

Then said Jacinto Treviño,
Taking a drink from a spring,
"Oh, what a poor bunch of Rangers;
They didn't do me a thing!"

Then said Jacinto Treviño,
"Now it is time to retire;

[1] HAM . . . BREAD: The Anglo-American addiction to the ham sandwich is much criticized in Border Mexican folklore.

I'm going to Rio Grande[2]
And I will welcome you there."

Now I must beg your permission,
This is the end of the chorus;
I am Jacinto Treviño,
A native of Matamoros.

[2] RIO GRANDE: Rio Grande City, on the Texas-Mexican border.

FOR DISCUSSION

1. You may have seen "western" movies which portray the Texas Rangers as heroes. How does the description of the Rangers in the "Corrido de Jacinto Treviño" differ from the Hollywood movie version? How would you account for the difference?

2. How do you think one of the Texas Rangers who encountered Treviño in Baker's Saloon would have described the incident? Do you think either his version or the description presented in the song would be strictly factual? What might this suggest about the study of history?

Jovita González

Born in Roma, close to Rio Grande City, Jovita González is a descendant of the first settlers of the area. One of the first Mexican-Americans to write in English about her own culture, she wrote for the annuals of the Texas Folklore Society in the 1920s. She taught in Texas for many years and was president of the Texas Folklore Society in the 1930s, the first Mexican-American to hold that post. In the following selections she tells about her land and her people.

Among My People

SHELLING CORN BY MOONLIGHT

In August, down towards the Rio Grande, the rays of the sun beat vertically upon the sandy stretches of land, from which all tender vegetation has been scorched, and the white, naked land glares back at the sun; the only palpitating things discoverable between the two poles of heat are heat devils. The rattlesnakes are as deeply holed up and as quiet as in midwinter. In the thickets of brush the roadrunners,[1] rusty lizards, mockingbirds, and all other living things pant. Whirlwinds dance across the stretches of prairie interspersed between the thickets of thorn. At six o'clock it is hotter than at midday. Seven o'clock, and then the sun, a ball of orange-pink, descends below the horizon at one stride. The change is

[1] ROADRUNNERS: birds of the cuckoo family.

magical. A soft cooling breeze, the pulmotor of the Border lands, springs up from the south.

Down in the *cañada,* which runs by the ranch, doves coo. Out beyond, cattle are grazing and calves are frisking. In the cottonwood tree growing beside the dirt "tank" near the ranch house the redbird sings. Children shout and play. From the corrals come the voices of vaqueros singing and jesting. Blended with the bleatings of goats and sheep are the whistles and hisses of the *pastor* (shepherd). The locusts complete the chorus of evening noises. Darkness subdues them; then, as the moon rises, an uncounted mob of mongrel curs set up a howling and barking at it that coyotes out beyond mock.

It was on a night like this that the ranch folk gathered at the Big House to shell corn. All came: Tío Julianito, the *pastor,* with his brood of sunburned half-starved children ever eager for food; Alejo the fiddler; Juanito the idiot, called the Innocent, because the Lord was keeping his mind in heaven; Pedro the hunter, who had seen the world and spoke English; the vaqueros; and, on rare occasions, Tío Esteban, the mail carrier. Even the women came, for on such occasions supper was served.

A big canvas was spread outside, in front of the kitchen. In the center of this canvas, ears of corn were piled in pyramids for the shellers, who sat about in a circle and with their bare hands shelled the grains off the cobs.

It was then, under the moonlit sky, that we heard stories of witches, buried treasures, and ghosts. I remember one in particular that sent chills up and down my spine.

"The night was dark, gloomy; the wind moaned over the treetops, and the coyotes howled all around. A knock was heard; the only occupant limped across the room and opened the door. A blast of cold wind put out the candle.

" 'Who is there?' he asked, looking out into a night as dark as the mouth of a wolf.

" 'Just a lost hermit,' answered a wailing voicc. 'Will you give a stranger a lodging for the night?'

"A figure wrapped in a black cape entered, and as he entered, a tomblike darkness and coldness filled the room.

" 'Will you take off your hat and cape?' the host asked solicitously of his mysterious guest.

" 'No—but—I shall—take off my head.' And saying this, the strange personage placed his head, a skull, upon the table nearby."

Then the *pastor* told of how he had seen spirits in the shape of balls of fire floating through the air. They were souls doing penance for their past sins. As a relief to our fright, Don Francisco suggested that Tío Julianito do one of his original dances to the tune of Alejo's fiddle. A place was cleared on the canvas, and that started the evening's merriment.

PEDRO THE HUNTER

Pedro was a wonderful person among all the people of the ranch. Besides being the most renowned hunter, he had seen the world, and conscious of his superiority, he strutted among the vaqueros and other ranch hands like an only rooster in a small barnyard. Besides, he spoke English, which he had learned on one of his trips up North. Yes, Pedro was a traveled man; he had been as far away as Sugar Land and had worked in the sugar-cane plantations. Many strange things he had seen in his travels. He had seen how the convicts were worked on the plantations and how they were whipped for the least offense. Yes, he, Pedro, had seen that with his own eyes.

He did not stay in the Sugar Land country long; the dampness was making him have chills. So he hired himself as a section hand. His auditors[2] should have seen that big black monster, *el Tren Volador.*[3] It roared and whistled and belched fire and smoke as it flew over the land. He would have liked being a section hand on the railroads had it not been for the food—cornbread and salt pork.

He had been told that if he ate salt pork, he would soon learn to speak English. Bah! What a lie! He had eaten it three times a day and had only learned to say "yes." But being anxious to see a city, he came to Houston. As he walked through the downtown streets one Saturday evening, he saw some beautiful American ladies singing at a corner. What attracted his attention was that they played the guitar. And that made him homesick for the ranch. He stopped to listen, and the beautiful ladies talked to him and

[2] AUDITORS: here, listeners.

[3] *el Tren Volador:* the Flying Train.

patted him on the back. They took him with them that night and let him sleep in a room above the garage. He could not understand them, but they were very kind and taught him to play the drum, and every evening the ladies, after putting on a funny hat, took the guitars and he the drum, and they went to town. They sang beautifully, and he beat the drum in a way that must have caused the envy of the passers-by, and when he passed a plate, many people put money in it. During the winter he learned English. But with the coming of spring he got homesick for the *mesquitales,* the fragrant smell of the *huisache,* the lowing of the cattle at sundown, and above all, for the mellow, rank smell of the corral. What would he not give for a good cup of black, strong ranch coffee, and a piece of jerky[4] broiled over the fire! And so one night, with his belongings wrapped up in a blanket, he left south by west for the land of his youth. And here he was again, a man who had seen the world but who was happy to be at home.

THE MAIL CARRIER

No people of the North feel cold more than do the Border people when the winter norther sweeps down. In the teeth of one of these northers we left Las Viboras ranch just before dawn, bound for the nearest railroad station, Hebbronville. The day proved to be as dreary as the dawn, and I amused myself counting the stiff jack rabbits that crossed our path. At a turn of the road the car almost collided with a forlorn-looking two-wheeled vehicle drawn by the sorriest-looking nag I had ever seen. On the high seat, perched like a bright-colored tropical bird, sat a figure wrapped up in a crazy quilt. On seeing us he stopped, motioned us to do the same, and in mumbled tones bade us good morning, asked where we were going, what might be the news at the ranches, and finally, were we all right. He seemed to ask these questions for the sake of asking, not waiting for a reply to any one of them. At last, having paused in his catechism[5] long enough for some sort of reply to be given, he put out one of his hands gingerly from under his brilliant cape to wave us good-bye.

[4] JERKY: meat, usually beef, cured by smoking or by drying in the sun.

[5] CATECHISM: here, long series of questions.

"That's Tío Esteban, the mail carrier," grandfather said. And that is how I met this employee of Uncle Sam. Six months later, suitcase and all, I rode with him twenty miles as a passenger, for the sum of two dollars and fifty cents. That summer we became intimate friends. He was the weather-beaten, brown-faced, black-eyed Cupid of the community. Often when some lovesick vaquero did not have a two-cent stamp to pay for the delivery of the love missive, he personally delivered the letter. Not only did he carry letters, but he served as secretary to those who could not write. He possessed a wonderful memory and could recite ballads and love poems by the hour. If the amorous outburst was in verse, his fee was double. He was a sly old fellow and knew all the love affairs of the community. I am not so sure of his honorableness as a mail carrier. I am afraid he sometimes opened the love missives. Once as he handed a love letter to Serafina, our cook, he said in a mellifluous[6] voice, "My dear Serafina, as the poet says, we are like two cooing doves." Poor Serafina blushed even to the whites of her eyes. Later she showed me that very phrase in the letter.

Tío Esteban knew not only all the love affairs but also all the scandal of the two counties through which he passed. And because of that, he was the welcome guest of every ranch house. He made grandfather's house his headquarters and could always have a bed with the ranch hands. He needed little encouragement to begin talking. He usually sat on a low stool, cleared his throat, and went through all the other preliminaries of a long-winded speaker. Ah, how we enjoyed his news! What did he care for what the papers said? They told of wars in Europe, of thousands of boys killed in the trenches, of political changes, of the Kaiser's surrender.[7] But what was all this compared with what Tío Esteban had to tell us?

Did we know Chon had left his wife because she did not wash her face often enough? And about Felipe's hog eating all the soap his wife had made? Pablo's setting hen, which had all white Leghorn eggs, had hatched all black chickens. A strange event, but not so strange if you remembered that Pablo's sister-in-law had black chickens. And with such news he entertained us until the roosters began to crow.

[6] MELLIFLUOUS (mə·lĭf'lo͞o·əs): honeyed.

[7] KAISER'S SURRENDER: surrender of the ruler of Germany to the Allied Powers.

THE PERENNIAL LOVER

"Las hijas de las madres que amé tanto
me besan ya como se besa un santo."

"The daughters of the mothers I loved so well
They kiss me now as they would kiss a saint."

Carlitos had made love to two generations of girls. As one crop of girls grew up to maidenhood, Carlitos declared his sentiments to each in turn. One by one they outgrew him, married, and had girls of their own. As the second crop came on, he remained ever-ready to offer his heart and hand to anyone who would listen to him.

He was not bad-looking. He was tall and lanky, and had it not been for his coconut head, pivoted on some eight inches of neck, his triangular ears, and big hands and splay feet, he would have been handsome. His moustache was the barometer for his emotions. When he was not in love, it hung limp and unkempt, but in the spring, when the world was aglow with prairie flowers and all Nature invited him to love, it was waxed and triumphant. I remember his coming to the ranch one day and calling my uncle aside most mysteriously.

"Look, Francisco," he said, displaying a package of ruled paper with carnations on one corner, "beautiful, isn't it? This year the carnations are bound to work. Last year I used violets and did not get a single answer. That's because violets do not inspire love; but wait until they see these carnations. I will get so many replies that it will be difficult for me to decide which girl I want. And look! This is what I am going to say."

Then he showed my uncle the circular which he sent every year, his declaration of love, for he always used the same, whether he sent it by mail or uttered it, one hand over his heart and eyes looking up to heaven for inspiration: "I can no longer bear the pain which devours my heart, and I would like to know whether my love is returned or not. Should I be so unfortunate as to be rejected, then I will put between us the immensity of the sea." But in spite of many rejections and more ignorings, he never left on his threatened voyages. He might for a few days go about in a mood suitable to a rejected lover, but he soon forgot.

One May, not long ago, I was back at the ranch and in the store when Carlitos entered. He was the most dejected-looking figure imaginable; his once beautiful moustache was the most melancholy part about him. Between sighs he told the clerk what he wanted. With another sigh he left the store.

"What's the matter with him?" I asked my uncle.

"Caught at last," he answered with a laugh. "Last spring, as usual, he distributed his love letters, and much to his astonishment, he was accepted by Lola, Tío Felipe's thirty-year-old daughter. When he opened the letter, I thought he had received a death notice. He turned as pale as a ghost, and I had to hold him up. When he had somewhat recovered, he said to me in a choking voice, 'Look, look.' I looked and read, 'I am greatly honored by your offer, which I am happy to accept with my father's consent.'

" 'I must congratulate you upon your good fortune,' I said, offering my hand.

" 'But you do not understand,' he said between sobs. 'I never meant to marry at all. I merely sent those letters because it gave me pleasure. Whatever shall I do in the spring now?' "

And this was spring, and his first year of married life.

TÍO PANCHO MALO

Tío Pancho Malo, they called him. After the fashion of these Mexican folk, the surname originated not from the fact that he was bad, but from the fact that he was different. No, he was not bad. He merely had his own queer notions, his own ideas which he followed in his own peculiar way. And unconformity with the general tendencies and general customs is sufficient to make anyone an outlaw amid any group of folk.

Tío Pancho was a philosopher, and like all philosophers, he was at outs with the world and his fellowmen. I knew him as an old toothless, wizened creature, weak physically, but mentally sharp and alert. He spoke very little then. But as I went through the Border country, I would often hear, "as Tío Pancho Malo did," or "as Tío Pancho Malo said." If he himself was not willing to speak, those who knew him were only too glad to tell you, and always with a laugh, concerning the old man and his idiosyncrasies.

As a young married man he had lived near Mier, in Mexico, on his few ancestral acres of worthless alkaline[8] land. "Bitter mesquites and poor folks' children are plentiful," is an old Border saying. And Tío Pancho's flock was more plentiful than the mesquite beans. His brood of boys were never bothered about keeping clean, for during the first two years of their life they were miniature Adams—except they wore no fig leaves—in a place far from being a Garden of Eden. When rebuked because of this indecency he permitted, he replied in a drawling voice, "Why should I interfere with the plans of my Creator? If he wanted children to wear clothes, he in his goodness would provide them."

When his wife died, she was buried without a coffin. "Who am I," he explained, "that I should prevent Nature from fulfilling her end? The sooner she mingles with Mother Earth, the sooner her destiny is fulfilled." After his wife's death he and his boys moved to Texas, where he became a *pastor* of goats. When the flock did not demand too much attention, he planted a few acres of land. One day, it is said, the ranch people were driven to hysterics by the appearance of his boys wearing gourds for hats.

"What is the object of a hat?" he asked. "Is it not protection from the elements? There in the shape of a gourd Nature has provided us with something that serves the same purpose and that does not cost anything."

He could neither read nor write; yet he composed poetry and expressed himself in a most flowery language. One day when he wanted an axe, he commanded one of his sons to bring him "that bright shiny object which man in his cruelty uses for the decapitation of defenseless trees."

When his boys grew up, his great exploit was the organization of a band. He did not know any music; neither did his sons. But what difference did that make? Their instruments were of the most rudimentary[9] forms: reed flutes, handmade guitars, an old fife, a trombone, cymbals, and a drum. As director, Tío Malo led this band from ranch to ranch, playing selections which they composed as the spirit moved them. Once they came to grandfather's ranch, and a more raggedy bunch I have never seen. They played a few

[8] ALKALINE (ăl′kə·lĭn): arid; containing mineral salts.

[9] RUDIMENTARY: here, simple; basic.

selections, at the end of which grandfather asked them if they played by note.

"No," Tío Pancho Malo replied, "we play for chickens, beans, corn, or whatever the rancheros may have, but we never require a note."

He was very proud of his sons' accomplishments as musicians, and often paid them compliments but never in their presence.

"My Tirso," he said confidentially to grandfather, "plays the trombone with the strength of an ox."

Tío Pancho Malo went up and down the river playing his music and expounding his theories. As the years passed and the boys married off, the band disbanded and Tío Pancho was left alone. The last I heard of him he was at Alice, Texas, where he eked out a living as a water carrier. He was brought before the court by the society for the prevention of cruelty to animals, accused of having ill-treated his donkey.

"Your Honor," he told the judge, "these good ladies have accused me of cruelty towards my donkey, saying that I make the poor skinny creature work. But these ladies have not stopped to consider that I also am poor, skinny, and have to work. The donkey and I live for each other. Without me he would starve; without him I would die of hunger. We work together, and for each other. One of us is not any good without the other. If these ladies prevent his working, both of us will starve, and that in my mind would be not only cruelty to animals but cruelty to me."

The court could do nothing but let Tío Pancho Malo go his way.

FOR DISCUSSION

1. It has been said that Mexicans are never happy away from their homelands in Mexico and the Southwest. Would Jovita González agree? Do you think this is a true reflection of the way Mexicans feel about their land?

2. Is Carlitos, the perennial lover, a distinctively "Mexican" character, or could he be found elsewhere? What about Pedro, the hunter? Tío Esteban, the mail carrier?

3. Was Pancho Malo a fool, or a wise man? Why do you think so?

Fermina Guerra

Fermina Guerra, a descendant of the early colonizers of the Rio Grande border, was born in the Laredo area. She studied at the University of Texas, where she wrote a master's thesis from which the following description of Rancho Buena Vista has been taken.

Rancho Buena Vista's interesting history and many traditions present a good idea of life on the frontier during the 1800s. While trying to establish homesteads, rancheros often had to face such perils as terrifying floods, bands of raiding Indians, and encounters with the much-feared Texas Rangers.

Rancho Buena Vista

Its Ways of Life and Traditions

In the northeastern part of Webb County, fifty miles from Laredo and twenty-one miles from Encinal, lies the Buena Vista Ranch. It is not large as ranches go, only about three thousand acres; but it has its share in the traditions of the ranch country.

The land is typical brush country. There is an abundance of prickly pear and other forms of cactus. Mesquite grass abounds, and in the lower places, foxtail and other tall grasses grow. In early times, the plains for twenty miles around were covered breast-high with *zacate de bestia*, but all this tall grass is gone now. The hardy bunch grasses best survive drouths and overgrazing.

The country is broken by many gravel hills, and the slopes are covered with fragments of petrified wood. From them a grotto twenty-five feet in length, six feet in width, and eight feet in height has been erected at the ranch house.

A stone's throw west of the ranch house flows a creek, generally a mere trickle of water interspersed with *esteros*, deep pools. In time of flood it overflows to cover a half-mile-wide valley and brings destruction in its wake. It rises in the high land to the south and empties into the Nueces River, eighteen miles to the north. Near its source, it is called El Pato (Duck), in its middle course, La Becerra (Heifer Calf), and near its mouth, La Parida, this last name meaning a female—perhaps a cow, perhaps a woman—with a newborn offspring.

The country is, comparatively speaking, newly settled. There had been ranches and towns along the Rio Grande since 1755, but in 1860, when Don Justo Guerra and his two sons, Florencio and Carmen, brought their herds of sheep and goats across the Rio Grande at Laredo, the country to the north was largely virgin land. There were not even resident Indians. Arrowheads and other Indian relics abound today, but the only Indians were raiding parties from farther north. The three Guerras came out to the Becerra Ranch, then owned by Casimiro Benavidez. At that time there were only four ranches in the region—El Pato, La Becerra, El Nido, and La Parida. Of them, only La Becerra remains.

After the Civil War broke out and the Southern ports were blockaded, the only outlet for cotton was through Mexico. One of the cotton roads from San Antonio to the Rio Grande was hacked out through the brush six miles north of La Becerra Ranch. The opening through the brush, now grass-covered, and the marks that the wide iron tires of the ox carts left on flint rocks in their path can yet be seen. While the guns of war thundered far away and ox carts rumbled across the Becerra, Don Justo Guerra, his wife, and their sons saw their herds increase. Ranching was the sole occupation of the country, and for most of these Border ranchers the war was as far away as the operations of Bismarck in Germany.[1] At the brandings, all the rancheros working in cooperation, the *orejanos*—the "slick ears," or mavericks—were held until the cow hunts were over. Then there was a roping contest, a kind of fiesta, at which the best ropers kept for their own the wild, unclaimed animals on which they contested. Sheep and wool,

[1] BISMARCK . . . GERMANY: Prince Otto von Bismarck (1815–1898) became prime minister of Prussia in 1862 and fought several wars with other European nations during the 1860s and 1870s.

however, for a long time were the chief products of the ranchers of this part of Texas.

Shortly after the close of the Civil War, Florencio Guerra married Josefa Flores from Laredo. He established himself farther down the creek at a natural rock ford. The banks were higher here, the creek deeper, the land more fertile. He named the place Buena Vista (Good View). Meanwhile, the country was being settled, and it became necessary to establish legal claim to the land under the Texas homestead law.

So much for the establishment of the Rancho Buena Vista. In time a school was built near the ranch house. Without presuming to domain or wealth, Buena Vista became a kind of social headquarters for the country around it. Yet the ways of life on it were characteristic of the ways of life on scores of other Mexican ranches between the Nueces and the Rio Grande, in the brush country of Texas—and also in the Border country of Mexico. The traditions pertaining to Buena Vista that have been told over and over among the children and grandchildren of Florencio Guerra and his wife, Josefa Flores, are the kind of traditions to be heard all up and down the Border country.

Some of them, perhaps a majority of them, treat of actual happenings, and are folklore only in that they are traditional and that they are hardly important enough for history. The stories are of Indians, floods, captives, sheepherders, buried treasure, violent death, happenings when the bishop came or the wool went to town. When a fire burns on a winter night or when it is raining and the water in Becerra Creek is high, people at Buena Vista tell and hear these traditions of the land.

HIGH WATER

Ever-present in the minds of ranch people is the question of water. The foremost topic of conversation among them is the condition of the range, the prospect of rain, the water of the tanks. This part of the country has never found good well water to pump up with windmills, and tanks are depended on for stock water.

In the old days there were no tanks. The cattle watered at the two or three creeks in the country. In time of drouth they were driven the eighteen miles to the Nueces River. There was never trouble over water rights. Through the years these ranchmen kept the peace among themselves; the struggle with Nature occupied their chief energies. The first fence went up in 1891. Don Florencio's son, Donato, used to go out of his way before and after school to watch the fence-building operations being carried on by the Callaghan Ranch hands, who were erecting a fence between Buena Vista Ranch and theirs.

Three times in the history of Buena Vista Ranch, La Becerra Creek has been half a mile wide—in 1878, 1903, and 1937. Of course, the oldest flood is the most romantic. Don Justo and his wife were still living then, old and set in their ways. Their ranch house was of mesquite poles and adobe, thatched with grass and set on the very banks of La Becerra Creek.

One day it started to rain; torrents poured down. As the creek began to rise and there was no abatement of the downpour, the other members of the family grew frightened. Not Don Justo. He had seen rain before; nothing ever came of it. But the rain poured all night and a second day; the creek continued to rise.

Now it was up to the corral, adjoining the house. No matter; it would go down presently. A second night, and a third day, the rain continued pouring. At dusk on the third day, the water began to enter the house. A young matron, wife of Don Carmen, holding her child in her arms, told her husband to take her to higher ground. She feared remaining in the house another night with that constantly rising water. Gladly enough, he complied. Before leaving, he begged his aged father and mother to accompany him, but they laughed. "You will get all wet for nothing," they said. "We have a roof over our heads. What if there is a little water in the house?"

But the young mother set out for the hill to the east. Before she reached it, she was obliged to swim to save herself and child, her husband aiding her. The rain was still pouring so hard that they got lost in the brush, but they went on eastward.

Eventually they found themselves on a well-known hill. Don Florencio's ranch was just a mile to the northwest. The mother asked her husband to go down there and ask for some dry clothing for the baby, as the night was cold and it was still raining hard. Willingly enough, Don Carmen set out.

On reaching the house, he told Don Florencio what had happened at the upper ranch. Hurriedly the latter saddled his best horse and set out to see what he could do to persuade his parents to leave their house and take to the hills. The water was not so high at Buena Vista, though it was at the door of the main house.

About daybreak, he reached the shore opposite his parents' ranch. There was a raging torrent between him and them. From afar off, barely to be seen among the treetops, he could discern the roof of the house and two people perched on it. He could hardly hear their feeble cries, so great was the distance.

Like most ranchmen of his time, Don Florencio could not swim. He depended upon his horse to carry him across streams. This task his present mount refused to perform. Time after time he forced the animal into the water, only to have it turn back. At length he returned to his own ranch for a fresh mount. This horse, too, refused to venture out into the flood. So Florencio was forced to flounder at the edge of the current and watch those faraway forms, fearing to see them disappear from sight. But towards evening, the waters began to recede, and the next day he was able to go out and rescue the exhausted old people from their predicament.

The flood of 1903 was unusual in that no rain accompanied it. One hot, sunny morning Don Florencio noticed what appeared to be a cloud of mist rising rapidly from the bushes south of the house along the creek. It was coming fast, with a rushing sound. Suddenly he realized that a wall of water, far wider than the creek banks, was bearing down upon him. One of his laborers was down the creek bed driving some goats to higher ground. Racing his horse, he hurried to get within calling distance of the man, Carlos. The laborer saw Don Florencio and heard his call, but not realizing that the danger was so close, went leisurely on with his work. Suddenly the turbulent water was upon him, and he was borne along with it as it swirled among the bushes. Fortunately, after his first fright, he was able to collect his wits sufficiently to grasp at an overhanging limb and so save his life.

The flood of 1937 was more prosaic; the creek itself did no particular damage, but the water destroyed all but three tanks in a radius of twenty miles and left the range worse off than before the rain.

Such is the life of the ranchmen of Southwest Texas; drouth and flood; too much water or not enough; then, now, and always.

INDIANS

Indians were not regular residents of the country, and no one knew from what tribe they came. It was generally believed that they were runaways from the Indian territory far to the north, for they were often dressed as white men and at first deceived their victims. By 1875 nearly all the Indians had been gathered into reservations by the U. S. Government, but it was customary to allow a few at a time to leave the reservations for the purpose of hunting. These would band together at some distance from the reservations and make forays to the south, where there were no soldiers to stop them.

Such bands occasionally made their way into the territory about Buena Vista Ranch. Don Florencio, in his boyhood, lived in constant fear of the Indians and often caused his father to laugh at him because he professed to have heard their whistling or cries in the brush or to have seen the dust sent up by their horses' hoofs.

The reports were not always figments of the imagination. Indians did come sometimes and had to be driven away. The oldest houses had apertures[2] in the walls, *troneras*, about four by twenty inches within the house and about three inches square on the outside, that gave opportunity for the besieged settler to fire in several directions without being in danger from Indian arrows. The whole countryside abounds in arrowheads. In a morning's walk one may pick up a hundred points of all sizes, ranging from delicate birdpoints to heavy arrowheads three inches or more in length.

The Indians came, though, chiefly to steal horses. They generally killed only in case of resistance. Don Florencio and his brother had worked too hard, in getting their horses, to stand idly by while the Indians drove them away. So one day when a band came upon them on the range—it was about 1877—Don Carmen and Don Florencio fired upon the band. The Indians had a number of horses with them; in return they fired a volley of arrows and several pistols, and Don Carmen's horse fell. His brother leaned down and lifted him to his own mount and then turned to fire at the Indians again. But the firing had startled the horses into flight, and the Indians took after them.

The fleeing horses ran toward the Buena Vista ranch house. From afar off one of the boys saw them coming and recognized

[2] APERTURES (ăp'ər•chərz): openings.

Indians in pursuit. He climbed up on the horse shed to see better. On came the horses. Just south of the ranch they swerved away toward the creek, at the edge of which old Marcos, the *pastor,* was herding the goats.

The boy began shouting to the women in the house below:

"Here come the Indians chasing horses!"

"They are coming here!"

"No, they are going to cross the creek south!"

"There are Marcos and the goats!"

"Now the Indians see Marcos!"

"He is stopping them! He is talking with them! They are quarreling!"

"Marcos is coming this way!"

"One of the Indians is aiming an arrow at him!"

"He's hit! The Indians are running on away down the creek after the horses! I think Marcos is dead!"

And he was. That visit was the last that the Indians made to Buena Vista Ranch.

Although the Indians did have firearms at this time, they used arrows on many occasions. They had used both pistols and arrows in the encounter earlier in the day, but on passing by the ranch, they killed Marcos with an arrow. They saw no need of wasting their ammunition.

LA CAUTIVA

Three miles south of Buena Vista Ranch was the ranch of Antonia Hinojosa, *la cautiva.* She was a romantic figure in the region, a former captive of the Indians. As a young woman she had lived in the Mexican state of Chihuahua. She had married young and had an infant son.

One day she went down to a creek near her hut to wash clothes and took her infant along. While she was there, a band of roving Indians from across the border came upon her and her child. They captured her, and cutting the ears off her son, left him lying on the creek bank. She never saw him again.

For a number of years she lived among the Indians, at length becoming the wife of one of them. By him she had a daughter, Lola. But she longed to escape. In a battle between tribes she was taken by the enemy and separated from her daughter. The Indian man grieved for her and told Lola the Spanish name of her mother and urged her to seek her if anything ever happened to him. Then it happened that Lola's Indian father was killed in a personal fight with another brave. In some way Lola escaped or got cut off from the Indians and grew up among white people. She never ceased searching for her mother, but it was many years before she found her.

Meanwhile, the mother, Antonia Hinojosa, had been released by the Indians because the United States Government made them give up all their captives. She came to La Becerra Creek and took up a homestead. She lived alone and often had not even a laborer to help her.

She made bags out of cowhides to carry away the earth she painstakingly dug out of the burrow pit of her tank; that little tank is still to be seen on her ranch.

Her ranch house was of stone, brought from the bed of La Becerra Creek. The stones are now part of a modern house on the neighboring ranch of Cesario Benavidez.

Once, during the Indian raids, she closed up her horses in her corral and herself mounted guard upon them day and night. When the Indians arrived, she stood her ground so that they left her unmolested.

Through a long life she had many trials and adventures. But she prospered. One of her laborers was the ill-fated victim of Justo Manta, the "badman" of the region. At length, when she was a feeble old woman, her daughter learned of her whereabouts. Lola was about sixty years old at the time and lived in Austin. She came alone to her mother's ranch, and thus they lived together for a few years.

The daughter decided to return to Austin, but she left word with friends and neighbors that they should advise her immediately if Antonia fell ill. Several years passed before the call came. Upon receiving word of her illness, Lola set out from Austin posthaste. But Antonia, being one hundred and five years old, did not live till her daughter arrived. Lola heard of her mother's death when she reached a ranch about five miles away.

The shock was too great for the aged traveler; she was unable to continue her journey. Soon she herself died, and the two are buried side by side on the ranch of "La Cautiva."

TÍO PEDRO AND THE RANGERS

Tío Pedro, a cousin to Don Florencio, had established himself on a small ranch to the north of Buena Vista. He was a peaceful man with a wife and two children. He worked hard and managed to gather together a stock of cattle and several good horses.

It happened that on one occasion three Mexican thieves stole some of his horses. He missed the animals almost immediately and began to search for them. After traveling for a little while through the brush, he saw their tracks in the dust and set out after the thieves. He came upon them about dusk as they were preparing their evening meal. Dismounting from his horse, he shouted to them to surrender his animals. Instead, they opened fire. He returned their fire, and one of the thieves fell dead. The others fled.

Much perturbed over what he had done, he traveled back to the ranch, where he arranged for the burial of the dead man. Then he went down to Cotulla and gave himself up to the authorities for trial. He was released on bond. At the time of his trial he was cleared. Returning to the ranch, he took up his peaceful life again.

A few months later, two Texas Rangers presented themselves at Buena Vista Ranch. These men were the terror of the Mexican ranch country. It was generally believed that they shot first and asked questions afterward. They were very civil and asked for Don Pedro Fulano, who had killed a horse thief in defense of his rights.

Don Florencio asked why the Rangers were seeking him. They laughingly replied that they had never seen a Mexican brave enough to stand up for his rights and would like to set eyes on one. As they were passing through the country on their rounds, this seemed a good opportunity to do so.

The tale did not ring true to Don Florencio. It was about dinner time; so he asked the strangers to remain for the meal, offering to take them over afterward. Much to his surprise, they stayed and chatted in a friendly way over the meal.

But Don Florencio was worried. Calling aside his young son, he said, "Saddle a horse, Donato, and ride to the ranch of Tío Pedro. Tell him the 'rinches' are here asking about the killing of the horse thief, and though they don't seem unfriendly, I want to warn him."

Donato sped away unmolested. When he reached Tío Pedro and gave his message, the man was between two fires. He had been tried and acquitted of his crime, but tales he had heard of the "rinches" made him fear that they would pay little attention to the laws of the country if they had inclinations otherwise.

For a while he stood in thought. Then he said to his wife, "I don't know these men. Maybe they mean no harm. But once they catch me, if they are out to get me, I will stand no chance of escaping. I'd better go now, while I am free."

Immediately he saddled a horse and rode away. Weeks later, after the Rangers had gone, his family received word from him saying he had reached safe haven in Old Mexico and for them to sell the property and join him.

This they did, and crumbling walls now attest to the terror of the "rinches" that lived in the hearts of even honest men.

FOR DISCUSSION

1. Describe the character and the qualities of the people who lived on the Rancho Buena Vista. How would the experiences described in this selection have helped to mold them?

2. What seemed to be the Rangers' opinion of the Mexicans? What opinion did the Mexicans have of the Rangers? Do you think each opinion was justified by past experience?

3. Do you think Tío Pedro did the right thing by running away? What do you think might account for the mistrust the Rangers and the Mexicans in the story felt toward each other?

Américo Paredes

b. 1915

Américo Paredes was born in Brownsville, Texas, on the Rio Grande border; he is descended from the settlers who colonized that area in 1749. He now teaches folklore and Mexican-American studies at the University of Texas, Austin.

Dichos

Proverbs have been called "the wisdom of many and the wit of one." They are "the wit of one" because it was some one person, at some particular time and place, who put the thought of each proverb into just the right words. To put something into "just the right words" is to create poetry, and the unknown persons who created proverbs were poets in their own right. Proverbs are "the wisdom of many" because they express the feelings and attitudes of whole groups of people rather than just the feelings of an individual. They are part of the literature of distinctive groups of people that we refer to as "folk." That is, proverbs are one of the basic forms of folk poetry, and a very ancient kind. Proverbs are found in the Old Testament, for example.

The formal word for "proverb" in Spanish is *refrán,* but most Mexicans and Mexican-Americans call them *dichos,* "sayings." They are a special way of saying things, of making a point, and they are used in ordinary conversation everywhere that Mexican-Americans speak to each other in Spanish, whether on a farm in South Texas or at a steel mill in Gary, Indiana. To those unfamiliar with the culture, the effect of *dichos* is to make the language "colorful." To the sayer of *dichos,* they are a time-honored way of expressing himself, of putting over a point in just the right way.

Dichos do not contain absolute truths; that is, they are not a set of rules telling one exactly how to behave at all times. They are a storehouse of good advice to be used according to specific situations. That is why two *dichos* may give opposite advice. This is also true of proverbs in English; for example, "Look before you leap" and "He who hesitates is lost."

There are two kinds of *dichos* most commonly used. One is called by folklorists the "true proverb." It is always a complete statement, a sentence. It is also a complete little poem, using the same kinds of effects that are found in other poetry. One of the simplest poetic effects, and perhaps the oldest, is balanced structure—the balancing of the two parts of the *dicho* on either side of a center, like two weights on an old-fashioned type of scales. For example: *Arrieros somos / y en el camino andamos.*[1] This is the same type of structure used in the Old Testament, in the Psalms: "The Lord is my shepherd; / I shall not want."

Contrast may be added to balanced structure, and the effect is even more pleasing. In the following *dichos* the two underlined words are contrasted with each other: *Mucho ruido / y pocas nueces; A buena hambre / no hay mal pan.* Another effect is made by adding rhyme, as in much poetry we are familiar with: *Cada oveja / con su pareja; A Dios rogando / y con el mazo dando.* Other *dichos* may use alliteration, the repetition of the first sounds of words, rather than the final sounds as in rhyme—"rough and ready." Alliteration is not common in Spanish poetry, but assonance is used very frequently. In assonance, only the vowel sounds are matched (*olas* and *hoja,* for example), instead of vowel and consonant sounds, as we do to make rhymes (*olas* and *solas*). The following *dicho* uses both assonance and alliteration: *Quien da pan a perro ajeno / pierde el pan y pierde el perro.*

The other kind of *dicho* is known as a "comparison." It is not a complete sentence, but a phrase beginning with the word *como,* "like." Most *dichos* of this kind have stories behind them, stories that everybody knows, so that when somebody says, "I was left

[1] English translations of the proverbs used as examples appear on following pages.

there like the man who whistled on the hill," everybody knows just how the speaker was left—holding the bag.

These *dichos* were collected by Américo Paredes and translated especially for this book.

TRUE PROVERBS

A buena hambre no hay mal pan.

No food is bad when you're good and hungry.

A Dios rogando y con el mazo dando.

Pray to God, but keep hammering away (at your problem).

¿A dónde ha de ir el buey, que no ha de seguir arando?

Where can the ox go that he will not have to plow? (Where can a poor man go, that he will not be given the hardest kind of job for the lowest pay?)

Ahora es cuando, yerbabuena, le has de dar sabor al caldo.

Now is the time, peppermint, when you must flavor the soup. (Now is the time to do or die; now or never; put up or shut up.)

Al pan, pan y al vino, vino.

Let us call bread, bread and wine, wine. (Be realistic.)

Arrieros somos y en el camino andamos.

We are all drovers,[2] traveling down the same road. (We are all the same, living in the same hard world; we are all in it together; the world is not so wide that we will not meet again.)

Cada oveja con su pareja.

Each ewe to its ram. (To each his own.)

[2] DROVERS: A drover drives livestock to market.

Cada quien en su casa, y Dios en la de todos.

Each man in his house, and God in all houses. (Let each man mind his own business, and God will smile on all of us.)

Caras vemos, corazones no sabemos.

We see their faces, but we do not know their hearts.

Como dueño de mi atole, lo menearé con el dedo.

Since the gruel is mine, I will stir it with my finger (if it pleases me).

Como quiera nace el maiz, estando la tierra en punto.

Nothing will keep the corn from growing, as long as the land is ready. (Nothing will stop us, if we have planned well.)

Cuando no hay lomo, de todo como.

When I can't have steak, I'll eat anything.

Cuando se pelean las comadres, salen las verdades.

When gossips fight, then truths will out.

Da y ten, y harás bien.

Give (some of your goods) and keep (a part), and you will do well.

El flojo y el mezquino andan dos veces el camino.

The sluggard and the miser travel the same road twice. (Lazy and stingy people do not give their all to what they do, so they often have to do it again.)

El pan ajeno hace al hijo bueno.

Another man's food will make your son good. (Going out into the world and earning his own keep makes a son more considerate of his parents.)

El perro que come huevos, aunque le quemen el pico.

You can't make a dog stop stealing eggs, even if you burn his mouth. (It is hard to make people change their ways.)

Él que carga su costal sabe lo que lleva dentro.

He who shoulders the bag knows what he carries in it. (No one really knows your troubles except yourself.)

Él que con lobos anda, a aullar se enseña.

He who runs with wolves will learn to howl. (If you run around with unsavory characters, you will pick up their ways.)

Él que ha de ser barrigón, aunque lo fajen.

If you're born with a big belly, a girdle won't be much help.

Él que nace pa' tamal, del cielo le caen las hojas.

If you're born to be a *tamal,* heaven will send you the cornshucks. (Tamales are made wrapped in cornshucks, so they go together like hamburgers and buns. You will be what you're going to be, and circumstances will conspire to keep you from being anything else.)

Él que no habla, Dios no lo oye.

If you don't speak up, God will not hear you. (You have to speak up for your rights, or you won't get them.)

Él que tiene más saliva traga más pinole.

The man with the most saliva eats the most *pinole.* (*Pinole* is a fine powder made from roasted corn and brown sugar. You cannot eat it with a dry mouth. "Them as has, gits." What you have, though, may be money, influence, ability, or persistence.)

Entre menos burros, más olotes.

The fewer donkeys, the more corncobs. (The fewer to share, the more to go around.)

Es poco el amor, ¡y gastándolo en celos!

So little love—why waste it in jealous quarrels? (Let us not waste the little we have.)

Haz bien, y no mires a quien.

Do good, without caring to whom.

Las cuentas claras y el chocolate espeso.

I like my accounts clear and my chocolate thick.

Lo pescaron en las tunas, con las manos coloradas.

They caught him in the prickly-pear patch, with his hands all red.

Los golpes hacen al buen vaquero.

Hard knocks make a good horseman.

Manso como un cordero, mientras hago lo que quiero.

I'm as gentle as a lamb, as long as I'm doing what I want to do.

Más vale pobre que solo.

It's better to be poor than to live alone.

Mucho ruido y pocas nueces.

Much noise and few nuts (harvested or shelled). (Much ado about nothing.)

No creas que la luna es queso, nomás porque la ves redonda.

Don't think the moon is made of cheese, just because you see it's round.

No hay que conejear sin perros.

Never go hunting rabbits without dogs. (Be prepared before you do something.)

No le hace que nazcan chatos, nomás que resuellen bien.

No matter if they (my children) are born with pug noses, as long as they can breathe all right. (No matter if my style is crude, as long as I get things done.)

No te fíes del mexicano que fuma puro, ni del gringo que te dice "compadre."

Never trust a Mexican who smokes a cigar, or a gringo who tells you he's your pal. (The cigar-smoking Mexican has become Americanized and no longer has the Mexican-American's interests at heart, while the supposedly friendly American just wants the Mexican's vote.)

Quien da pan a perro ajeno, pierde el pan y pierde el perro.

If you feed somebody else's dog, you're out of food and still have no dog. (Don't waste your efforts on impossible things.)

Todo cabe en un jarrito, sabiéndolo acomodar.

You can put anything into a jar, if you know how to pack it in. (Nothing is impossible.)

Un clavo saca otro clavo, o los dos se quedan dentro.

A nail can be used to drive out another nail, unless both stay in the wood. (Emergencies require emergency measures, but sometimes they do not work.)

Vale más mal conocido, que mejor por conocer.

A known evil is better than an uncertain good. (Stay with what you have; don't go chasing wild geese.)

Ya comí, ya bebí, ya no me encuentran aquí.

I have eaten, I have drunk; I will not be here for long. (Sometimes said jokingly by a guest who has to eat and run. But it may also be said of a person who has received favors from another and then no longer shows his face at his friend's house.)

COMPARISONS

Como agua pa' chocolate.

Like water for making chocolate. (Very hot, that is. When someone is very angry, he is "like water for making chocolate.")

Como atole de enfermo.

Like a sick man's gruel. (This is all a sick man is fed, so it stands for something that is very boring, that you just can't stand any more.)

Como calcetín de a nicle.

Like a five-cent pair of socks. (*Nicle* is a Mexican-Americanism for *nickel.* When you don't like something, you say it fits you "like a five-cent pair of socks.")

Como el burro del aguador (or *del zacatero*).

Like the water seller's (or the hay seller's) burro. (The poor burro carries water or hay on his back all day, for sale, but he never gets any of it. When you are close to something you want very much but cannot have it, you say you are like the water seller's burro.)

Como el que chifló en la loma.

Like the man who whistled on the hill. (There is a story about several thieves or smugglers who posted one man on a hill as a lookout. The lookout was supposed to whistle, to warn them if police were coming. But the others saw the police officers before the lookout did, and they ran away. When the lookout saw the officers, he began to whistle as loudly as he could; but nobody answered him. So he kept whistling and whistling until he was caught.)

FOR DISCUSSION

1. What kind of wisdom is expressed in *dichos?*

2. Can you find *dichos* in the list that give similar advice? Are there some that give opposite advice?

3. How many can you pick out that use contrast as a poetic device?

4. Make a list of some Mexican *dichos* or American proverbs you may have heard outside of class.

Even more than Jacinto Treviño, Gregorio Cortez became the folk hero of all Mexican-Americans in Texas. Cortez was twenty-six years old in 1901, when a Texas sheriff killed Cortez's brother when trying to arrest him for a crime he had not committed. Gregorio Cortez killed the sheriff while trying to protect his brother. He became a fugitive, chased by many posses of enraged Anglo-Texans. For ten days Cortez eluded pursuit, riding more than four hundred miles from central Texas to the Rio Grande border near Laredo. On the way he had a gunfight with a posse and killed a second Texas sheriff. Exhausted from his ride, Cortez was captured before he could cross the border into Mexico.

The legal battle in Cortez's behalf lasted almost four years. He was finally acquitted of murder for the death of the first sheriff, but he was sentenced to life imprisonment for the killing of the second. Efforts in his behalf continued, and he was ultimately pardoned in 1913.

To all Mexican-Americans, Cortez became a symbol of the man who fights for his rights. This selection, from the book With His Pistol in His Hand, *attempts to reproduce part of the story of Gregorio Cortez as Mexican-American rancheros told it to Dr. Paredes.*

The Legend of Gregorio Cortez

They still sing of him—in the cantinas and the country stores, in the ranches when men gather at night to talk in the cool dark, sitting in a circle, smoking and listening to the old songs and the tales of other days. Then the *guitarreros* sing of the Border raids and the skirmishes of the men who lived by the phrase "I will break before I bend."

They sing with deadly serious faces, throwing out the words of the song like a challenge, tearing savagely with their stiff, calloused fingers at the strings of the guitars.

And that is how, in the dark quiet of the ranches, in the lighted noise of the saloons, they sing of Gregorio Cortez.

After the song is sung, there is a lull. Then the old men, who have lived long and seen almost everything, tell their stories. And when they tell about Gregorio Cortez, the telling goes like this:

HOW GREGORIO CORTEZ CAME TO BE IN THE COUNTY OF EL CARMEN

He was a man, a Border man. What did he look like? Well, that is hard to tell. Some say he was short and some say he was tall; some say he was Indian brown and some say he was blond like a newborn cockroach. But I'd say he was not too dark and not too fair, not too thin and not too fat, not too short and not too tall; and he looked just a little bit like me. But does it matter so much what he looked like? He was a man, very much of a man; and he was a Border man. Some say he was born in Matamoros; some say Reynosa; some say Hidalgo County on the other side. And I guess others will say other things. But Matamoros, or Reynosa, or Hidalgo, it's all the same Border; and short or tall, dark or fair, it's the man that counts. And that's what he was, a man.

Not a gunman, no, not a bravo.[1] He never came out of a cantina wanting to drink up the sea at one gulp. Not that kind of man, if you can call that kind a man. No, that wasn't Gregorio Cortez at all. He was a peaceful man, a hard-working man like you and me.

He could shoot. Forty-four and thirty-thirty, they were the same to him. He could put five bullets into a piece of board and not make but one hole, and quicker than you could draw a good deep breath. Yes, he could shoot. But he could also work.

He was a vaquero, and a better one there has not ever been from Laredo to the mouth. He could talk to horses and they would understand. They would follow him around, like dogs, and no man knew a good horse better than Gregorio Cortez. As for cattle, he could set up school for your best *caporal.* And if an animal was lost and nobody could pick up a trail, they would send for Gregorio Cortez. He could always find a trail. There was no better tracker

[1] BRAVO: fierce or ill-tempered man.

in all the Border country, nor a man who could hide his tracks better if he wanted to. That was Gregorio Cortez, the best vaquero and range man that there ever was.

Gregorio Cortez was not of your noisy, hell-raising type. That was not his way. He always spoke low, and he was always polite, whoever he was speaking to. And when he spoke to men older than himself, he took off his hat and held it over his heart. A man who never raised his voice to parent or elder brother, and never disobeyed. That was Gregorio Cortez, and that was the way men were in this country along the river. That was the way they were before these modern times came and God went away.

He should have stayed on the Border; he should not have gone up above, into the North. But it was going to be that way, and that was the way it was. Each man has a certain lot in life, and no other thing but that will be his share. People were always coming down from places in the North, from Dallas and San Antonio and Corpus and Foro West. And they would say, "Gregorio Cortez, why don't you go north? There is much money to be made. Stop eating beans and tortillas and that rubbery jerked beef. One of these days you're going to put out one of your eyes; pull and pull with your teeth on that stuff and it suddenly lets go. It's a wonder all you Border people are not one-eyed. Come up above with us, where you can eat white bread and ham."

But Gregorio Cortez would only smile, because he was a peaceful man and did not take offense. He did not like white bread and ham; it makes people flatulent and dull. And he liked it where he was. So he always said, "I like this country. I will stay here."

But Gregorio Cortez had a brother, a younger brother named Román. Now Román was just like the young men of today, loud-mouthed and discontented. He was never happy where he was, and to make it worse, he loved a joke more than any other thing. He would think nothing of playing a joke on a person twice his age. He had no respect for anyone, and that is why he ended like he did. But that is yet to tell.

Román talked to Gregorio and begged him that they should move away from the river and go up above, where there was much money to be made. And he talked and begged so, that finally Gregorio Cortez said he would go with his brother Román, and they saddled their horses and rode north.

Well, they did not grow rich, though things went well with them because they were good workers. Sometimes they picked cotton, sometimes they were vaqueros, and sometimes they cleared land for the Germans. Finally they came to a place called El Carmen, and there they settled down and farmed. And that was how Gregorio Cortez came to be in the county of El Carmen, where the tragedy took place.

ROMÁN'S HORSE TRADE AND WHAT CAME OF IT

Román owned two horses, two beautiful sorrels[2] that were just alike, the same color, the same markings, and the same size. You could not have told them apart, except that one of them was lame. There was an American who owned a little sorrel mare. This man was dying to get Román's sorrel—the good one—and every time they met, he would offer to swap the mare for the horse. But Román did not think much of the mare. He did not like it when the American kept trying to make him trade.

"I wonder what this gringo thinks," Román said to himself. "He takes me for a fool. But I'm going to make him such a trade that he will remember me forever."

And Román laughed a big-mouthed laugh. He thought it would be a fine joke, besides being a good trade. There were mornings when the American went to town in his buggy along a narrow road. So Román saddled the lame sorrel, led him a little way along the road, and stopped under a big mesquite that bordered on the fence. He fixed it so the spavined[3] side was against the mesquite. Román waited a little while, and soon he heard the buggy coming along the road. Then he got in the saddle and began picking mesquites off the tree and eating them. When the American came around the bend, there was Román on his sorrel horse. The American stopped his buggy beside Román and looked at the horse with much admiration. It was a fine animal, exactly like the other one, but the American could not see the spavined leg.

[2] SORRELS: reddish-brown horses.

[3] SPAVINED: afflicted with a disease which enlarges or stiffens the joint of a horse's hind leg.

"Changed your mind?" the American said.

Román stopped chewing on a mesquite and said, "Changed my mind about what?"

"About trading that horse for my mare."

"You're dead set on trading your mare for this horse of mine?" Román said.

"You know I am," the American said. "Are you ready to come round?"

"I'm in a trading mood," said Román. "With just a little arguing you might convince me to trade this horse for that worthless mare of yours. But I don't know; you might go back on the deal later on."

"I never go back on my word," the American said. "What do you think I am, a Mexican?"

"We'll see, we'll see," said Román. "How much are you willing to give in hand?"

"Enough to give you the first square meal you've had in your life," the American said.

Román just laughed, and it was all he could do to keep from guffawing. He knew who was getting the best of things.

So they made the deal, with Román still sitting on his spavined horse under the tree, chewing on mesquites.

"Where's the mare?" Román said.

"She's in my yard," said the American, "hung to a tree. You go get her and leave the horse there for me, because I'm in a hurry to get to town."

That was how Román had figured it, so he said, "All right, I'll do it, but when I finish with these mesquites."

"Be sure you do, then," the American said.

"Sure, sure," said Román. "No hurry about it, is there?"

"All right," the American said, "take your time." And he drove off leaving Román still sitting on his horse under the mesquite, and as he drove off, the American said, "Now isn't that just like a Mexican. He takes his time."

Román waited until the American was gone, and then he stopped eating mesquites. He got off and led the horse down the road to the American's yard and left him there in place of the little sorrel mare. On the way home Román almost fell off his saddle a couple of times, just laughing and laughing to think of the sort of face the American would pull when he came home that night.

The next morning when Gregorio Cortez got up, he said to his brother Román, "Something is going to happen today."

"Why do you say that?" asked Román.

"I don't know," said Gregorio Cortez. "I just know that something is going to happen today. I feel it. Last night my wife began to sigh for no reason at all. She kept sighing and sighing half the night, and she didn't know why. Her heart was telling her something, and I know some unlucky thing will happen to us today."

But Román just laughed, and Gregorio went inside the house to shave. Román followed him into the house and stood at the door while Gregorio shaved. It was a door made in two sections; the upper part was open, and Román was leaning on the lower part, like a man leaning out of a window or over a fence. Román began to tell Gregorio about the horse trade he had made the day before, and he laughed pretty loud about it, because he thought it was a good joke. Gregorio Cortez just shaved, and he didn't say anything.

When what should pull in at the gate but a buggy, and the American got down, and the Major Sheriff of the county of El Carmen got down too. They came into the yard and up to where Román was leaning over the door, looking out.

The American had a very serious face. "I came for the mare you stole yesterday morning," he said.

Román laughed a big-mouthed laugh. "What did I tell you, Gregorio?" he said. "This gringo has backed down on me."

Just as the words came out of Román's mouth, the sheriff whipped out his pistol and shot Román. He shot Román as he stood there with his head thrown back, laughing at his joke. The sheriff shot him in the face, right in the open mouth, and Román fell away from the door, at the Major Sheriff's feet.

And then Gregorio Cortez stood at the door, where his brother had stood, with his pistol in his hand. Now he and the Major Sheriff met, each one pistol in hand, as men should meet when they fight for what is right. For it is a pretty thing to see, when two men stand up for their right, with their pistols in their hands, front to front and without fear. And so it was, for the Major Sheriff also was a man.

Yes, the Major Sheriff was a man; he was a gamecock[4] that had won in many pits, but in Gregorio Cortez he met a cockerel that pecked his comb. The Major Sheriff shot first, and he missed; and Gregorio Cortez shot next, and he didn't miss. Three times did they shoot, three times did the Major Sheriff miss, and three times did Gregorio Cortez shoot the sheriff of El Carmen. The Major Sheriff fell dead at the feet of Gregorio Cortez, and it was in this way that Gregorio Cortez killed the first sheriff of many that he was to kill.

When the Major Sheriff fell, Gregorio Cortez looked up, and the other American said, "Don't kill me; I am unarmed."

"I will not kill you," said Gregorio Cortez. "But you'd better go away."

So the American went away. He ran into the brush and kept on running until he came to town and told all the other sheriffs that the Major Sheriff was dead.

Meanwhile, Gregorio Cortez knew that he too must go away. He was not afraid of the law; he knew the law, and he knew that he had the right. But if he stayed, the Rangers would come, and the Rangers have no regard for law. You know what kind of men they are. When the governor of the state wants a new Ranger, he asks his sheriffs, "Bring all the criminals to me." And from the murderers he chooses the Ranger, because no one can be a Ranger who has not killed a man. So Gregorio Cortez knew that the best thing for him was to go away, and his first thought was of the Border, where he had been born. But first he must take care of his brother, so he put Román in the buggy and drove into town, where his mother lived.

Now there was a lot of excitement in town. All the Americans were saddling up and loading rifles and pistols, because they were going out to kill Cortez. When all of a sudden, what should come rolling into town but the buggy, driven by Gregorio Cortez. They met him on the edge of town, armed to the teeth, on horseback and afoot, and he on the buggy, holding the reins lightly in his

[4] GAMECOCK: rooster trained for cockfighting.

hands. Román was in the back, shot in the mouth. He could neither speak nor move, but just lay there like one who is dead.

They asked him, "Who are you?"

And he said to them, "I am Gregorio Cortez."

They all looked at him and were afraid of him, because they were only twenty or twenty-five, and they knew that they were not enough. So they stepped aside and let him pass and stood talking among themselves what would be the best thing to do. But Gregorio Cortez just drove ahead, slowly, without seeming to care about the men he left behind. He came to his mother's house, and there he took down his brother and carried him in the house. He stayed there until dawn, and during the night groups of armed men would go by the house and say, "He's in there. He's in there." But none of them ever went in.

At dawn Gregorio Cortez came out of his mother's house. There were armed men outside, but they made no move against him. They just watched as he went down the street, his hands resting on his belt. He went along as if he was taking a walk, and they stood there watching until he reached the brush, and he jumped into it and disappeared. And then they started shooting at him with rifles, now that he was out of pistol range.

"I must get me a rifle," said Gregorio Cortez, "a rifle and a horse."

They gathered in a big bunch and started after him in the brush. But they could not catch Gregorio Cortez. No man was ever as good as him in hiding his own tracks, and he soon had them going around in circles, while he doubled back and headed for home to get himself a rifle and a horse.

HOW GREGORIO CORTEZ RODE THE LITTLE SORREL MARE ALL OF FIVE HUNDRED MILES

He went in and got his thirty-thirty, and then he looked around for the best horse he had. It is a long way from El Carmen to the Border, all of five hundred miles. The first thing he saw in the corral was the little sorrel mare. Gregorio Cortez took a good look at her, and he knew she was no ordinary mare.

"You're worth a dozen horses," said Gregorio Cortez, and he saddled the little mare.

But by then the whole wasps' nest was beginning to buzz. The President of the United States offered a thousand dollars for him, and many men went out to get Gregorio Cortez. The Major Sheriffs of the counties and all their sheriffs were out. There were Rangers from the counties, armed to the teeth, and the King Ranch Rangers from the Capital, the meanest of them all, all armed and looking for Cortez. Every road was blocked and every bridge guarded. There were trackers out with those dogs they call hounds, that can follow a track better than the best tracker. They had railroad cars loaded with guns and ammunition and with men, moving up and down trying to head him off. The women and children stayed in the houses, behind locked doors; such was the fear they all had of Gregorio Cortez. Every town from the Capital to the Border was watching out for him. The brush and the fields were full of men trying to pick up his trail. And Gregorio Cortez rode out for the Border, through brush and fields and barbed-wire fences, on his little sorrel mare.

He rode and rode until he came to a great broad plain, and he started to ride across. But just as he did, one of the sheriffs saw him. The sheriff saw him, but he hid behind a bush, because he was afraid to take him on alone. So he called the other sheriffs together and all the Rangers he could find, and they went off after Gregorio Cortez just as he came out upon the plain.

Gregorio Cortez looked back and saw them coming. There were three hundred of them.

"We'll run them a little race," said Gregorio Cortez.

Away went the mare, as if she had been shot from a gun, and behind her came the sheriffs and the Rangers, all shooting and riding hard. And so they rode across the plain, until one by one their horses foundered and fell to the ground and died. But still the little mare ran on, as fresh as a lettuce leaf, and pretty soon she was running all alone.

"They'll never catch me like that," said Gregorio Cortez, "not even with those dogs called hounds."

Another big bunch of sheriffs rode up, and they chased him to the edge of the plain, and into the brush went Cortez, with the trackers after him, but they did not chase him long. One moment there was a trail to follow, and next moment there was none. And the dogs called hounds sat down and howled, and the men scratched their heads and went about in circles looking for the trail. And Gregorio Cortez went on, leaving no trail, so that people thought he was riding through the air.

There were armed men everywhere, and he could not stop to eat or drink, because wherever he tried to stop, armed men were there before him. So he had to ride on and on. Now they saw him, now they lost him, and so the chase went on. Many more horses foundered, but the mare still ran, and Gregorio Cortez rode on and on, pursued by hundreds and fighting hundreds every place he went.

"So many mounted Rangers," said Gregorio Cortez, "to catch just one Mexican."

It was from the big bunches that he ran. Now and again he would run into little ones of ten or a dozen men, and they were so scared of him that they would let him pass. Then, when he was out of range, they would shoot at him, and he would shoot back at them once or twice, so they could go back and say, "We met up with Gregorio Cortez, and we traded shots with him." But from the big ones he had to run. And it was the little sorrel mare that took him safe away, over the open spaces and into the brush, and once in the brush, they might as well have been following a star.

So it went for a day, and when night fell, Cortez arrived at a place named Los Fresnos and called at a Mexican house. When the man of the house came out, Cortez told him, "I am Gregorio Cortez."

That was all he had to say. He was given to eat and drink, and the man of the house offered Gregorio Cortez his own horse and his rifle and his saddle. But Cortez would not take them. He thanked the man, but he would not give up his little sorrel mare. Cortez was sitting there, drinking a cup of coffee, when the Major Sheriff of Los Fresnos came up with his three hundred men. All the other people ran out of the house and hid, and no one was left in the house, only Gregorio Cortez, with his pistol in his hand.

Then the Major Sheriff called out, in a weepy voice, as the *corrido* says. He sounded as if he wanted to cry, but it was all done to deceive Gregorio Cortez.

"Cortez," the Major Sheriff said, "hand over your weapons. I did not come to kill you. I am your friend."

"If you come as my friend," said Gregorio Cortez, "why did you bring three hundred men? Why have you made me a corral?"

The Major Sheriff knew that he had been caught in a lie, and the fighting began. He killed the Major Sheriff and the second sheriff under him, and he killed many sheriffs more. Some of the sheriffs got weak in the knees, and many ran away.

"Don't go away," said Gregorio Cortez. "I am the man you are looking for. I am Gregorio Cortez."

They were more than three hundred, but he jumped their corral, and he rode away again, and those three hundred did not chase him any more.

He kept riding on and on, by day and by night, and if he slept, the mare stood guard, and she would wake him up when she heard a noise. He had no food or cigarettes, and his ammunition was running low. He was going along a narrow trail with a high barbed-wire fence on one side and a nopal[5] thicket on the other, and right before he hit a turn, he heard horses ahead. The first man that came around the turn ran into Gregorio Cortez with his pistol in his hand. There was a whole line of others behind the first, all armed with rifles, but they had to put the rifles away. Then Gregorio Cortez knocked over a tall nopal plant with his stirrup and made just enough room for his mare to back into while the Rangers filed by. He stopped the last one and took away his tobacco, matches, and ammunition. And then he rode away.

He rode on to La Grulla, and he was very thirsty, because he had not had water in a long time, and the mare was thirsty too. Near La Grulla there was a dam where the vaqueros watered their stock. But when Gregorio Cortez got there, he saw twenty armed men resting under the trees that grew close to the water. Gregorio Cortez stopped and thought what he could do. Then he went back into the brush and began rounding up cattle, for this was cattle country and steers were everywhere. Pretty soon he had two hundred head, and he drove them to water, and while the cattle drank, he and the mare drank too. After he had finished, some of the Rangers that were resting under the trees came over and helped him get the herd together again, and Gregorio Cortez rode off with the herd, laughing to himself.

[5] NOPAL: type of cactus.

He rode on and on, and by now he knew that the Rio Grande was near. He rode till he came to Cotulla, and there he was chased again. The little mare was tired, and now she began to limp. She had cut her leg and it was swelling up. Gregorio Cortez rode her into a thicket, and the Rangers made him a corral. But once in the brush, Gregorio Cortez led the mare to a coma tree and tied her there. He unsaddled her and hung the saddle to the tree, and he patted her and talked to her for a long while. Then he slipped out of the thicket, and the Rangers didn't see him because they were waiting for him to ride out. They waited for three days, and finally they crept in and found only the mare and the saddle.

HOW EL TECO SOLD GREGORIO CORTEZ FOR A MORRAL FULL OF SILVER DOLLARS

Gregorio Cortez was gone. While all the armed men were guarding the thicket where the mare was tied, he walked into Cotulla itself. He walked into town and mixed with the Mexicans there. He sat on the station platform and listened to other men while they talked of all the things that Gregorio Cortez had done. Then he went to a store and bought himself new clothes and walked out of the town. He went to the river and took a bath and then swam across, because the bridge was guarded. That sort of man was Gregorio Cortez. They don't make them like him any more.

He had only three cartridges left, one for one pistol and two for the other, and he had left his rifle with the mare. But he was very near the Rio Grande, and he expected to cross it soon. Still, he needed ammunition, so he walked into El Sauz and tried to buy some, but they did not sell cartridges in that town. Then he thought of trying some of the houses, and chose one in which there was a pretty girl at the door, because he knew it would be easier if he talked to a girl. There was not a woman that did not like Gregorio Cortez.

The girl was alone, and she invited him into the house. When he asked for ammunition, she told him she had none.

"My father has taken it all," she said. "He is out looking for a man named Gregorio Cortez."

Gregorio Cortez was embarrassed because he could see that the girl knew who he was. But she did not let on and neither did he.

He stayed at the house for a while, and when he left, she told him how to get to the Rio Grande by the quickest way.

Now all the people along the river knew that Gregorio Cortez was on the Border, and that he would soon cross, but no one told the sheriffs what they knew. And Gregorio Cortez walked on, in his new clothes, with his pistols in a *morral,* looking like an ordinary man, but the people he met knew that he was Gregorio Cortez. And he began to talk to people along the way.

Soon he met a man who told him, "You'll be on the other side of the river tonight, Gregorio Cortez."

"I think I will," he said.

"You'll be all right then," said the man.

"I guess so," said Gregorio Cortez.

"But your brother won't," the man said. "He died in the jail last night."

"He was badly wounded," said Gregorio Cortez. "It was his lot to die, but I have avenged his death."

"They beat him before he died," the man said. "The Rangers came to the jail and beat him to make him talk."

This was the first news that Gregorio Cortez had heard, and it made him thoughtful.

He walked on, and he met another man who said, "Your mother is in the jail, Gregorio Cortez."

"Why?" said Gregorio Cortez. "Why should the sheriffs do that to her?"

"Because she is your mother," the man said. "That's why. Your wife is there too, and so are your little sons."

Gregorio Cortez thought this over, and he walked on. Pretty soon he met another man who said, "Gregorio Cortez, your own people are suffering, and all because of you."

"Why should my own people suffer?" said Cortez. "What have I done to them?"

"You have killed many sheriffs, Gregorio Cortez," said the man. "The Rangers cannot catch you, so they take it out on other people like you. Every man that's given you a glass of water has been beaten and thrown in jail. Every man who has fed you has been hanged from a tree branch, up and down, up and down, to make him tell where you went, and some have died rather than tell. Lots of people have been shot and beaten because they were your people. But you will be safe, Gregorio Cortez; you will cross the river tonight."

"I did not know these things," said Gregorio Cortez.

And he decided to turn back and to give himself up to the governor of the state so that his own people would not suffer because of him.

He turned and walked back until he came to a place called Goliad, where he met eleven Mexicans, and among them there was one that called himself his friend. This man was a vaquero named El Teco, but Judas should have been his name. Gregorio Cortez was thirsty, and he came up to the eleven Mexicans to ask for water, and when El Teco saw Gregorio Cortez, he thought how good it would be if he could get the thousand-dollar reward. So he walked up to Cortez and shook his hand and told the others, "Get some water for my friend Gregorio Cortez."

Then El Teco asked Gregorio Cortez to let him see the pistols he had, and that he would get him some ammunition. Gregorio Cortez smiled, because he knew. But he handed over the guns to El Teco, and El Teco looked at them and put them in his own *morral*. Then El Teco called the sheriffs to come and get Gregorio Cortez.

When Gregorio Cortez saw what El Teco had done, he smiled again and said to him, "Teco, a man can only be what God made him. May you enjoy your reward."

HOW GREGORIO CORTEZ WENT TO PRISON . . . FOR KILLING THE SHERIFFS

When the sheriffs came to arrest Gregorio Cortez, he spoke to them and said, "I am not your prisoner yet. I will be the prisoner only of the governor of the state. I was going to the Capital to give myself up, and that is where I'll go."

The sheriffs saw that he was in the right, so they went with him all the way to the Capital, and Cortez surrendered himself to the governor of the state.

Then they put Cortez in jail, and all the Americans were glad, because they no longer were afraid. They got together and they tried to lynch him. Three times they tried, but they could not lynch Gregorio Cortez.

And pretty soon all the people began to see that Gregorio Cortez was in the right, and they did not want to lynch him any more. They brought him gifts to the jail, and one day one of the judges came and shook the hand of Gregorio Cortez and said to him, "I would have done the same."

But Gregorio Cortez had many enemies, for he had killed many men, and they wanted to see him hanged. So they brought him to trial for killing the Major Sheriff of the county of El Carmen. The lawyer that was against him got up and told the judges that Cortez should die because he had killed a man. Then Gregorio Cortez got up, and he spoke to them.

"Self-defense is allowed to any man," said Gregorio Cortez. "It is in your own law, and by your own law do I defend myself. I killed the sheriff, and I am not sorry, for he killed my brother. He spilled my brother's blood, which was also my blood. And he tried to kill me too. I killed the Major Sheriff defending my right."

And Gregorio Cortez talked for a long time to the judges, telling them about their own law. When he finished, even the lawyer who was against him at the start was now for him. And all the judges came down from their benches and shook hands with Gregorio Cortez.

The judges said, "We cannot kill this man."

They took Gregorio Cortez all over the state, from town to town, and in each town he was tried before the court for the killing of a man. But in every court it was the same. Gregorio Cortez spoke to the judges, and he told them about the law, and he proved that he had the right. And each time the judges said, "This man was defending his right. Tell the sheriffs to set him free."

And so it was that Gregorio Cortez was not found guilty of any wrong because of the sheriffs he had killed. And he killed many of them, there is no room for doubt. No man has killed more sheriffs than did Gregorio Cortez, and he always fought alone. For that is the way the real men fight, always on their own. There are young men around here today who think that they are brave. Dangerous men they call themselves, and it takes five or six of them to jump a fellow and slash him in the arm. Or they hide in the brush and fill him full of buckshot as he goes by. They are not men. But that was not the way with Gregorio Cortez, for he was a real man.

FOR DISCUSSION

1. Do you think Gregorio Cortez should have avenged his brother's death by killing the sheriff? Whom would you hold responsible for the deaths which followed?

2. Did Gregorio Cortez do the right thing when he allowed himself to be captured by the sheriffs?

3. Why is Gregorio Cortez so important and beloved a figure in Mexican-American folklore?

Guitarreros

Black against twisted black
The old mesquite
Rears up against the stars
Branch bridle hanging,
While the bull comes down from the mountain
Driven along by your fingers,
Twenty nimble stallions prancing up and down the *redil* of
the guitars.
One leaning on the trunk, one facing–
Now the song:
Not cleanly flanked, not pacing,
But in a stubborn yielding that unshapes
And shapes itself again,
Hard-mouthed, zigzagged, thrusting,
Thrown, not sung,
One to the other.
The old man listens in his cloud
Of white tobacco smoke.
"It was so," he says,
"In the old days it was so."

FOR DISCUSSION

The man in the poem ponders the passing of the old days. What does he miss? What ideas and attitudes of the present day would bother him?

Josephina Niggli

b. 1911

Josephina Niggli was born in Monterrey, Mexico, not far from the villages she has written about. Her family left Mexico during the revolution when she was less than three years old. She attended school in San Antonio and was graduated from the College of the Incarnate Word, where she won several writing prizes. She now lives in Chapel Hill, North Carolina, and teaches writing at the University of North Carolina.

Miss Niggli's stories, set in old Mexico, deal with the lives of everyday working people. "The Street of the Three Crosses" and "The Engagement" humorously portray the courtship of Porfirio the miser and Alma Orona. "The Street of the Cañon" is a variation of a well-known Mexican folktale in which an innocent young girl dances with the devil. Miss Niggli's understanding of human nature is evident in these tales, where the trials of everyday living are treated with dignity and humor. Her play Sunday Costs Five Pesos *dramatizes certain comical aspects of male and female relationships in a small Mexican village.*

The Street of the Three Crosses

He who eats with his nose, pays with his mouth.
Mexican proverb

The moon hung like a silver crescent behind the blue belfry of the pink church, and the sky was night indigo with a silver sheen. At the four corners of the Plaza of Independence hung oil lanterns, throwing their small circles of yellow light on the broad cement walk.

Beyond this walk, in the center of the plaza, the bitter orange trees were heavy with fruit; the limes were in blossom, and their sweet perfume drenched the music-filled air—for the orchestra was playing in the bandstand.

Clusters of women moved counterclockwise on the street side; the men clockwise on the orchestra side. Some of the older people sat on benches, or on straight chairs hired from the "Sunday Evening Plaza Chair Association," a concern owned by Porfirio, the carver of wood, Pepe Gonzalez, and Andrés Treviño.

Although the orchestra conductor was urging his men to play as loudly as possible, the shrill voices of the plaza crowd were louder still. Above the noise rose the high tones of the candymaker, calling his wares: "Almond paste, nut cheese, candies of burnt milk, of sweet potato, of cactus heart. Who will buy my candies? Almond paste! Nut cheese!" And when he paused, the town gardener would take up the refrain with, "Carnations, roses, gardenias! Buy flowers for your mother, your sister, your sweetheart, your wife! Carnations for her mouth, roses for her heart, gardenias for her hair!"

As the gardener wandered through the crowd, his white trousers flapping around his thin brown legs and his straw hat set well back on his head to show he was an honest man, Porfirio stopped him.

"Eh, Don Serapio, give me a small gift of flowers."

The old man chuckled, tipping his head to one side. "A gift, is it? Wood is your trade, flowers mine. Let me see the color of your money."

"Now, Don Serapio," Porfirio protested, "you know I am a poor soul. I have not the wealth of Pepe Gonzalez, that son of a cheese factory. One little gift of flowers is not much to ask."

Don Serapio rolled his eyes toward heaven and ran his tongue over his teeth. His tray needed mending, and he had intended to take it to Porfirio the next day. That job would cost about fifty centavos. A bouquet of flowers cost ten centavos. . . .

He beamed and said, "Listen to me, Porfirio. Every man knows the worth of his own blanket. This tray of mine needs mending. In exchange for such labor I will give you a bouquet of flowers. Is it agreed?"

Porfirio answered eagerly, "But naturally, Don Serapio. Bring your tray tomorrow. And now I want your most beautiful gardenia—one with a very loud smell."

For forty centavos' profit, the gardener handed over a waxen white flower. As Porfirio hurried across one of the cement paths, Don Serapio chuckled and fell into step with Don Nacho. It was whispered in the town that because of his great stomach, the mayor had not seen his own feet for the past ten years.

"That Porfirio," said Don Serapio, and recounted the little episode. He finished with, "Someday he will learn that his fine deals always lose him money. Much cheaper to pay out the coins and be done with it. Forty centavos that ten-centavo flower cost him, but Porfirio thinks he got it for nothing. What a magnificent intellect."

"Flowers," said Don Nacho thoughtfully. "So Porfirio makes deals for flowers, does he? And for whom were the flowers?"

Don Serapio's mouth dropped open. "I never thought to ask him!" He slapped his palm against his forehead. "San Benedito,[1] is it possible that Porfirio, that tightfisted man, is rolling the eye at some girl?"

When Don Nacho laughed, his stomach quivered in sympathy. "And you the finest gossip in Hidalgo. Every man knows the worth of his own blanket, you said!" Still laughing, he passed on with the crowd.

Porfirio found his friend Andrés Treviño walking with Nena Santos and Alma Orona. He knew that to join them was impossible.

[1] SAN BENEDITO: St. Benedict.

Two boys and two girls walking together would create a scandal. But sitting in a chair beside her mother was Don Nacho's homely daughter, Chela. He hurried to her and whispered. She nodded, and a moment later joined the promenade. Porfirio sat impatiently beside Doña Mariliria, waiting for the group of three girls and a boy to encircle the plaza and return to where he was sitting, so that no gossip could connect his name with Chela's.

He sat very straight on one of his own chairs, the gardenia tightly gripped in his hot palm.

"That is a pretty flower," said Don Nacho's fragile wife.

Porfirio smiled weakly at her. If she continued to admire it, he, of politeness, must offer it to her, and he knew enough of women to know she would not refuse.

"It is a poor thing," he said quickly. "Already it is wilting."

"Do you like gardenias?" she asked with a mischievous gleam in her eye. She wondered what excuse he would make to keep from giving it to her. Porfirio's love of money was famous not only in Hidalgo, but through all the five villages strung along the banks of the Sabinas River.

"The little doctor," he said hastily, "tells me that gardenia perfume is very good for weakness of the chest."

"Have you a weakness of the chest?"

Porfirio squirmed on the hard straight chair. "No, not exactly. But I might have. Better to prevent sickness than to pay doctors' bills."

"Indeed, yes," said Doña Mariliria, hiding a smile behind her large black net fan and winking at Pepe Gonzalez, who came up to them.

"Eh, Porfirio, have you paid for that chair?"

"Why should I pay for it? I own it."

"Not that chair," said Pepe, with a sly glance at Doña Mariliria. "That one belongs to me. Your chairs are on the other side of the plaza."

"Come now, Pepe, is this a kind thing? Do not you and Andrés and I own all the chairs? Besides, the money would go to the Association. Why should I pay money to myself?"

"And steal the rightful share that belongs to Andrés and myself?" Pepe flung up his hands in a scandalized gesture. "I ask you, Doña Mariliria, is that fair, is that honest? Every Sunday night we divide the profits between us in three equal sections. Is it right that one should have more than the other two?"

"But I don't have more than you," Porfirio snapped. "If the money is not there at all, how can I have more nothing than you do? That is foolish."

Doña Mariliria tapped him on the arm with her fan. "But if you were not sitting in the chair, someone else would sit on it, paying ten centavos for the privilege. In that way you deprive your partners of three and one-half centavos each."

"A small amount, true," said Pepe. "But if all of us sat in our chairs, how could we make a profit?"

Porfirio sprang to his feet. "There is your chair," he cried. "It is cheaper to stand. Soon you will be charging me for the air I breathe!"

At this moment he saw his group coming toward him, and with a curt bow to Doña Mariliria, he hurried to join them. With careful management he contrived to walk between Chela and Alma Orona. To his prejudiced eyes Chela's homeliness, her large nose, heavy black brows, and wide, full-lipped mouth, pointed up the serene prettiness of Alma, with her large clear eyes, her heavy black hair worn in a crown of braids, and her skin warmed by the sun to a dark gold.

The gardenia slipped from his fingers to Alma's. She gave him a quick sideways glance, and he said with careful innocence, "Don Nacho says the moon will be late tonight."

Andrés Treviño said, "Pablo the goatherd told me that a late moon gives the goats moon madness."

There was a gasp of protest from Nena Santos. "Andrés Treviño! And you a good Christian talking to Pablo the goatherd! Have you no care for your soul, and he the son of Grandfather Devil?"

While Andrés was trying to explain to Nena that it was impossible to be a goat owner without having traffic with goatherds, Porfirio asked Alma if she would be at her window later in the evening.

"If you come with musicians," she whispered wickedly.

"*Ay*, but Alma, musicians cost money."

"So! Am I so worthless then?" With a toss of her head she separated herself from the group and walked away with Chela. Nena gave a little scream at finding herself alone with two men and darted after them. Andrés and Porfirio stared moodily at each other.

"That Nena Santos," Andrés mourned. "Why is it given to a man to be afflicted by a stubborn woman?"

"To your own troubles," retorted Porfirio, moving toward the bandstand. "I have enough of my own."

But Don Alonso, the orchestra leader, who knew Porfirio's bargaining ways, was adamant. To play the rooster[2] cost five pesos. It had always cost five pesos, and he did not see why it should be cheaper for the woodcarver.

"But five pesos," Porfirio wailed, "is a lot of money for thirty minutes' work. And when the music is done, what do I have left?"

"The smiles of a woman," said Don Alonso promptly, who had often parried this argument. "That should be enough for any man."

"Five pesos," mourned Porfirio. "*Ay* me, that is a fortune—a very fortune."

"For two pesos," said Don Alonso, "I could give you a guitar and a violin. But a proper rooster is played with five men. Of course, if you want your girl to think herself worth only two pesos. . . ."

Porfirio shuddered. Alma Orona was as proud as the mountains. If she thought he put her value so low, she would never speak to him again. And he loved Alma Orona. He really loved her. He loved her more than the two hundred pesos he had saved to buy her trousseau and rebuild a house and shop for their married life. But during the time he had saved those two hundred pesos, he had not counted upon all the extra money it seemed a courtship needed. For example, these five pesos, thrown, as it were, on a musical wind.

"I can't pay five pesos," he cried desperately. "I can't, Don Alonso."

Don Alonso looked over his shoulder at his musicians and winked. As one man they winked back at him.

"In the new casino they are building," said Don Alonso smoothly, "it would be a nice thing to have an orchestra-stand at the far end of the patio, as I have told you many times."

"But the committee says it would be a useless extravagance."

[2] PLAY THE ROOSTER: serenade a young woman.

"The committee lacks a musical soul. Should you erect such a platform. . . ."

"But that would take lumber!"

"Of course," said Don Alonso, shrugging his unconcern, "if you prefer to pay us five silver pesos cash, we will be glad to play. . . ."

"One moment," said Porfirio, wrinkling his forehead in a desperate endeavor to think. "One little moment. I have some lumber left over from the making of two coffins. It might be possible—it might be just possible."

"A stand," said Don Alonso, "to seat seven men, and sufficient room for me to walk about."

"At the southern end of the patio . . . yes," said Porfirio, "it is possible. And you will play for me?"

"In return for a really fine stand," said the harp player, "perhaps we could excel ourselves and give you all of us tonight."

"All of you," Porfirio breathed happily, looking around at the seven faces—eight, with Don Alonso. "Including the drum?"

"Including," said Don Alonso grandly, "the saxophone."

It seemed to Porfirio that time moved slowly forward to the hour of the serenade. The free benches were occupied, and he was afraid to sit in one of his own chairs for fear Pepe Gonzalez or Andrés Treviño would demand payment of him. His legs ached from standing, and he was thankful when Bob Webster[3] invited him to his house for a glass of wine.

"To the ending of a year," Bob said in toast, and Porfirio echoed him.

"So you are leaving Hidalgo, Don Bob?"

"At this hour next month I will be on the blue Gulf."

"*Ay,* that will be a grand thing. But the valley will miss you."

Bob said with an air of surprise, "And I will miss the valley. Sometimes I almost wish I didn't have to leave."

Bob poured another glass of sherry for Porfirio.

"Enough, enough," murmured the young man. "Already my brain clouds, and I will have no words to speak to Alma Orona. Wine makes me stupid and sleepy."

"A *tequilito,* perhaps?"

[3] BOB WEBSTER: American who had come to Hidalgo to run the cement quarry.

"Thank you, Don Bob, but—well, a little one. This is my first playing of the rooster. I shake with nerves."

Bob laughed and gave him a small glass of tequila. Porfirio poured some salt on his palm, licked it, tossed the tequila down his throat, and ended by sucking a lemon. "Wine is for women," he said firmly, "but tequila puts heart in a man."

He rose and solemnly embraced Bob. "My good friend, when you leave Hidalgo, I will light a candle for you. I will even weep a little." With a formal bow, he walked steadily out of the house to meet Don Alonso and the orchestra members.

The men grouped themselves near the house of Alma Orona on the Street of the Three Crosses. Pepe Gonzalez had come along to offer his advice.

"Now, Porfirio, you stand there beneath the window. Don Alonso, the musicians, and I will stand across the street."

Porfirio looked at his friend suspiciously. "But that window belongs to the house of old Don Ursulo. Alma Orona's is there."

"Nonsense! How can you tell the difference?"

"By the color. Alma's house is pink and green. Don Ursulo's is blue and red."

"'By the color,' he says." Pepe turned to the musicians. "At night he thinks he can tell the difference in color. Has he not remarkable eyes? And only today I was reading in a book that under moonlight nothing has color—nothing."

"I don't care," said Porfirio stubbornly. "I'm not going to play the rooster in front of the wrong house."

Don Alonso said gravely, his eyes twinkling behind his thick-lensed glasses, "There is a true way to distinguish the houses. Only this afternoon Don Ursulo said that of all pieces, his favorite was the North American jazz piece 'Yes, We Have No Bananas.' If we play it, it will bring him purring to the door. Then we will know to whom the window belongs."

"A most excellent idea," said Pepe, who had heard Don Ursulo on the subject of bananas.

Porfirio, his head buzzing from the effects of the tequila and wine, rolled his eyes from Pepe's face to Don Alonso's. Although Pepe was his very good friend, Porfirio never quite trusted him. But at last he nodded his head. "Very well. Play the jazz. We will see what happens."

"But first," said Pepe quickly, "you are too far from the window. Stand closer so that you can hear Alma's sighs. Remember, she is too shy a maiden to open the window immediately. Oh, and take off your hat, Porfirio. You are serenading a young lady, not drinking beer in the saloon."

When Porfirio was placed to Pepe's satisfaction, the cheese-maker's son hastily retired to the safety of the musicians' group. At a nod from Don Alonso, the violins released a wailing note of warning; then the harp added its rippling sound, the drums and flutes joined in; and finally the precious saxophone, ordered from a North American mail-order house and entrusted to Don Alonso's fifteen-year-old son, took up the melody. "Yes, We Have No Bananas" ricocheted down the narrow Street of the Three Crosses.

Suddenly the window was flung open. Old Don Ursulo, in lavender nightgown and bright pink nightcap, swung up a pail of water and flung it with full force over Porfirio's head. The woodcarver, his mouth open ready to voice lovers' phrases, stood immobile in surprise, the water running down his face and dripping from his shoulders. The music came to a jerking pause.

As Porfirio slowly turned around, musicians, Don Alonso, and Pepe Gonzalez whirled and ran up the street, stumbling and pushing against each other, harp, guitars, and violins clutched for safety against their owners' stomachs. They did not pause for breath until they were safely crouching behind the bar in the Saloon of the Devil's Laughter. Then Pepe emitted a choked snort, and they pounded each other's backs and laughed until the tears came.

But Porfirio, left alone, water dripping in a pool about his feet, was not laughing. He slowly put on his hat and trudged home, his heels dragging in the dirt. He realized with mournful certainty that his playing of the rooster for Alma Orona had entered the pages of Hidalgo's history.

FOR DISCUSSION

1. Porfirio is a miser, but does he really save any money? How does his miserly behavior affect his standing in the community?

2. Many writers (including Miss Niggli) argue that Mexicans are not as money-conscious or as greedy as Americans. Discuss this view. Does an apparent disregard for money mean that a person is not ambitious?

The Engagement

Alma's father and mother greeted their guests with much ceremony that afternoon. Doña Juanita Perez, the boardinghouse keeper, came early, secretly elated at having Bob Webster for escort. The little doctor, Don Nacho, Father Zacaya, and Don Rosalío arrived in a body, as befitted the dignity of the four rulers of Hidalgo.

They sat in the narrow oblong living room on stiff cane chairs, Doña Juanita Perez enthroned in a rocker, and Alma's parents side by side on the settee. Above their heads a large mirror framed in gold reflected the tan lace curtains at the window, the oval photograph of Don Carlos and Doña Triumfa in their wedding clothes, and the round table, covered with an embroidered cloth, which supported an oil lamp of hand-painted china displaying purple morning glories and dark red pansies.

Don Carlos served the men small glasses of very sweet wine, while the women drank cups of steaming hot chocolate flavored with cinnamon sent in by Alma from the kitchen, for Alma, as a modest girl, was not permitted to be present.

Finally, from the hall, came the sound of muted voices. The little doctor tiptoed forward and cautiously opened the door. They could hear Andrés Treviño say plaintively, "My feet hurt. Your shoes are too small for me, Pepe." And Pepe's lofty answer, "Your mind should be on the sufferings of Porfirio, not on your feet."

The little doctor slid the door against the jamb and turned around. His eyes were dancing with devilish delight. "How long shall we make them wait?" he whispered.

Don Rosalío lifted his white beard with one hand, and with the other drew a large gold watch from his vest pocket. "Do you think fifteen minutes would be too long?"

"Andrés is perspiring. Pepe is very pale," warned the little doctor.

Doña Juanita Perez smothered a laugh with a large green handkerchief. "My father made my first husband's petitioners wait over an hour."

Doña Triumfa tossed her head with disdain. "Your father, who was also mine, Juanita, was a man of wicked humor. But wicked!"

"He was that," said Don Carlos gloomily. "He kept my friends waiting nearly that long. I never forgave him for it."

"Eh," rumbled Don Nacho, "but what use to be old if we cannot have amusement at the expense of youth? What say you, Don Bob?"

Bob grinned. "I feel sorry for Porfirio, but Pepe Gonzalez needs a good dose of humility."

Once more the wine and chocolate were passed around. The liquid slid down throats with careful slowness.

Doña Juanita's curiosity could stand the suspense no longer. "Look at the poor innocents again, little doctor," she ordered.

The door opened for the space of an inch, and Pepe's voice said, "This black suit is too hot. I should have worn my white one. I am sweating like a mule."

"But black is more dignified than white," answered Andrés's clear tenor.

"A theory. A mere theory."

"They bury you in black," said Andrés, "and what could be more dignified than being buried?"

The door closed quickly, and the little doctor leaned against it, shaking with merriment.

"Haven't we punished them enough?" quavered Doña Triumfa, wiping the laughter tears from her eyes.

The men had stuffed their handkerchiefs in their mouths to deaden the sound of their mirth. Doña Juanita Perez had both hands clasped tightly across her lips, and her rocker was shaking under her heaving body.

Don Rosalío examined his watch again. "We've kept them twenty minutes. Let them in, little doctor."

Handkerchiefs were quickly returned to pockets, and the assembly was very dignified as the two young men supported each other into the room, each trying to hide behind the other. Their stiff collars were obviously too tight, and on both foreheads there were beads of perspiration. The little doctor returned to his chair, and the various eyes seemed, in Pepe's imagination, to swim together and form one great lidless eye, as hypnotic as a coiled snake's. He cleared his throat and glassily fixed his gaze on Don Carlos Orona's face.

"We are here . . ." he squeaked. He paused, swallowed an Adam's apple that seemed to have enlarged to twice its normal size, and began again at a more natural pitch. "We are here in the name of our good friend Porfirio Rodriguez, known to Hidalgo as the carver of wood. This fine friend is famous for his—for his . . ." he paused with an agonized glance at Andrés Treviño.

Andrés smiled vacantly, shrugged with a helpless gesture, and then suddenly realizing what was wanted of him, he pulled a much-folded paper from his hatband. With his tongue caught between his teeth, he carefully unfolded it and skimmed his eyes over the penciled words, smudged from constant handling. "Famous for his sobriety, steadiness of character, lack of vices, and. . . ."

"I know the rest of it," Pepe said with irritation. He looked again at Don Carlos Orona. "This fine friend is famous for his steadiness of character, lack of vices, and his great honesty. It is true knowledge that his worldly goods are few, but his parsimony. . . ."

"Care of money!" hissed Andrés.

"Care of money," said Pepe meekly into a chorus of sudden coughs, "identifies him as being a man well able to face the future free of monetary difficulties. With an established sum of two hundred pesos, he proposes to rebuild and furnish a house one block north of the Plaza of Independence on the street known as the Avenue of Illustrious Men. This house will face the back of the Church of Our Lady of the Miraculous Tear. . . ."

"Why, that's just down the street from me," said the little doctor cheerfully. "When Alma has her babies, I have only to run. . . ."

The concerted stare of everyone, including Pepe and Andrés, stopped the sentence. The little doctor twitched his bushy eyebrows, coughed, and hastily examined the heavy watch chain that hung suspended across the lower part of his chest.

Pepe looked at Andrés again, who prompted, "This house will face. . . ."

Pepe said, "This house will face the back of the Church of Our Lady of the Miraculous Tear, and will consist of four rooms, a patio, and a workshop at the back. Also from the two hundred pesos Porfirio proposes to buy a fine satin dress with wax orange blossoms, a pair of white kid shoes, and a long net veil, as well as a wedding bouquet of appropriate dimensions. With these offerings, our friend Porfirio Rodriguez. . . ."

Andrés said quickly with a strangled gasp, "You forget the two down pillows for kneeling at the church, two tall candles for the altar, and the marriage sums to Father Zacaya for the church ceremony and to Don Genaro for the civil wedding."

"Those matters can be taken for granted," said Pepe, who was growing irritated by the interruptions. He continued, "With these offerings, our friend Porfirio Rodriguez, the carver of wood, humbly asks in marriage the hand of the gracious and beautiful Señorita Alma Orona, the first banns[1] for this wedding to be sung in the church on Sunday morning next."

The words ended on a long sigh of relief. Pepe stepped backward until he was in line with Andrés. Both young men bowed from the waist, clapped their hats to their heads, and managed to walk backward through the door without falling over each other. They then turned and ran to the Saloon of the Devil's Laughter, where Porfirio, that young man famous for sobriety, steadiness of character, and lack of vices, was imbibing five-cent glasses of beer to aid his waiting. Pepe ordered two ten-cent glasses and glared at his friend. "It's over!" he said harshly. "Twenty minutes they made us wait—twenty minutes! An hour of my life disappeared with each minute."

"He kept wanting to leave," said Andrés, lifting his face from the glass, a line of foam marking his upper lip. "He said when it came your turn to ask for him, he hoped they kept you waiting five hours. Who are you going to ask for?" he added, turning to Pepe.

"Oh, I don't know," said Pepe lightly. "Probably some girl from the Valley of the Three Marys."

"The Valley of the Three Marys!" shrieked Andrés. When he saw the other customers and Don Dionisio, the saloonkeeper, looking at him, he hastily lowered his voice to a loud whisper. "The Three Marys' men would kill you.[2] Wouldn't they kill him, Porfirio?"

"I hope they do," said Porfirio, mournfully ordering another glass of beer. "Death is better than all this waiting."

"You've had enough beer," said Don Dionisio. "Soon you will be too drunk to go the plaza tonight. Besides, you owe me thirty centavos."

[1] banns: announcement of an intended marriage.

[2] The Three Marys' . . . kill you: There was a long-standing feud between the people of Hidalgo and those of the Valley of the Three Marys.

"Thirty centavos!" gasped Porfirio. "How can you do this to me, to me—your good friend? Did I not repair your shelves when that fool Dorotéo Lozano thought he was a ball and bounced against them?"

"For which I paid you two fine silver pesos," said Don Dionisio firmly.

"But the perfection of the job—the fine precision with which I swung the hammer on each nail head . . . is such artistry to cost but a mere two pesos? And now you want to charge me thirty centavos. . . ."

"Seventy centavos," said Pepe.

"Seventy?" whispered Porfirio. "He said thirty! I heard him say thirty!"

"But Andrés and I each had a glass," Pepe pointed out. "At ten cents a glass. That's seventy centavos, isn't it, Don Dionisio?"

"And five centavos extra for washing the glasses," said Don Dionisio, promptly. "Those large glasses take extra labor for the washing. After all, they are twice as large as the small ones. That makes the full sum seventy-five centavos."

"Seventy-five centavos!" Porfirio clutched the bar's edge and shut his eyes. He stood there a moment, his jaw clenched in silent agony. Then he shrieked, whirled, and rushed out of the saloon, a wave of laughter tumbling after him. Don Dionisio drew two more foaming glasses and set them in front of Pepe and Andrés. Then he drew another for himself. They lifted the glasses in toast. "To marriage," sighed Don Dionisio. "The poor fool should have guessed I would charge him nothing. I remember when I was waiting for my own proposal to be accepted. Such agony should not come to any man."

"That Porfirio and his money," said Andrés solemnly. "Someday someone will take five pesos from him, and they will not be joking. And that will be a sad day."

"True words," said Don Dionisio. "I wonder when that day will come?"

The men shrugged and drank their beer.

That night on the plaza, Porfirio arrived before Don Alonso and the orchestra were settled. They argued amiably over whether Porfirio still owed the orchestra platform. Porfirio contended no, because the rooster was never played. Don Alonso said yes, because the intention was good, and it was not his fault that Porfirio had stood under the wrong window. They finally settled the matter by Don Alonso's agreeing to play for nothing at the wedding feast, provided the family Orona agreed to take Porfirio as a son-in-law.

During this argument the plaza filled with people. News of Porfirio's request for Alma's hand had spread through the town, and good-luck wishes were called to him. No matter how much they teased him, the villagers were fond of the woodcarver and knew him to be excellent husband timber. Not so wealthy, of course, as the wild Pepe Gonzalez, heir to the cheese factory, which seemed to curd gold as well as milk. Don Timotéo Gonzalez contended that once Pepe settled down, any woman would be proud to call him husband, but Pepe's quick wit and mischievous humor had been felt by too many fathers to make him a favorite bachelor. It was rumored that many a parent's daily prayer ended with, "and please do not give me Pepe Gonzalez for a son-in-law." And as for Andrés Treviño—well, Andrés had loved Nena Santos for many years.

Yes, Porfirio had been the mothers' hope of Hidalgo, and now he had chosen Alma Orona. Well, Alma was a good girl. And a good worker. Did she not wash the clothes for Don Rosalío, yes, and for Bob Webster? There were many who felt that perhaps Porfirio was not quite good enough for her. He had not yet encountered that moment of testing of the soul when his true value would be stamped upon him. But in spite of village doubt, tonight Alma's and Porfirio's fates were to be solved.

The family Orona appeared on the plaza in a compact group. Porfirio, with much clearing of the throat, went up to them. Don Carlos spoke about the weather. Doña Triumfa expressed the hope that the spring rains would be heavy enough to help Don Rosalío's orange trees. Alma sat on the end of the bench, her eyes staring fixedly at the ground, saying nothing. At last Doña Triumfa said, lazily fanning herself, "Why do you two young people not walk around the plaza? Leave conversation to the old ones."

The ordeal was over. Porfirio gave a grin of relief and extended his arm to Alma. With a shy smile, she laid her fingers on his pink sleeve. As she rose and turned to walk with him, Don Alonso, in a fine burst of friendship, ordered the orchestra to play the beautiful "Song of Dolores Guerrero" which came out of Durango in 1840:

"To you, girl of the beautiful black hair,
Of the amber skin,
Of the great eyes and ardent gaze,
Of the proud head and sweet voice—
To you will I offer my love,
And to no other."

Scattered voices over the plaza took up the song. Soon the whole plaza was singing as Porfirio and Alma, proud as two children, walked around the great square three times, and thus formally announced their engagement to the village and the Sabinas Valley.

FOR DISCUSSION

Compare the Mexican style of courtship described in this story with what you believe is the typical American style. What are some advantages and disadvantages of each?

The Street of the Cañon

To the best cook goes the whole tomato.
Mexican proverb

It was May, the flowering thorn was sweet in the air, and the village of San Juan Iglesias in the Valley of the Three Marys was celebrating. The long dark streets were empty because all of the people, from the lowest-paid cowboy to the mayor, were helping Don Roméo Calderón celebrate his daughter's eighteenth birthday.

On the other side of the town, where the Cañon Road led across the mountains to the Sabinas Valley, a tall slender man, a package clutched tightly against his side, slipped from shadow to shadow. Once a dog barked, and the man's black suit merged into the blackness of a wall. But no voice called out, and after a moment he slid into the narrow, dirt-packed street again.

The moonlight touched his shoulder and spilled across his narrow hips. He was young, no more than twenty-five, and his black curly head was bare. He walked swiftly along, heading always for the distant sound of guitar and flute. If he met anyone now, who could say from which direction he had come? He might be a trader from Monterrey, or a buyer of cows' milk from farther north in the Valley of the Three Marys. Who would guess that an Hidalgo man dared to walk alone in the moonlit streets of San Juan Iglesias?

Carefully adjusting his flat package so that it was not too prominent, he squared his shoulders and walked jauntily across the street to the laughter-filled house. Little boys packed in the doorway made way for him, smiling and nodding to him. The long, narrow room with the orchestra at one end was filled with whirling dancers. Rigid-backed chaperones were gossiping together, seated in their straight chairs against the plaster walls. Over the scene was the yellow glow of kerosene lanterns, and the air was hot with the too-sweet perfume of gardenias, tuberoses, and the pungent scent of close-packed humanity.

The man in the doorway, while trying to appear at ease, was carefully examining every smiling face. If just one person recognized him, the room would turn on him like a den of snarling mountain-cats, but so far all the laughter-dancing eyes were friendly.

Suddenly a plump, officious little man, his round cheeks glistening with perspiration, pushed his way through the crowd. His voice, many times too large for his small body, boomed at the man in the doorway. "Welcome, stranger, welcome to your house." Thrusting his arm through the stranger's, and almost dislodging the package, he started to lead the way through the maze of dancers. "Come and drink a toast to my daughter—to my beautiful Sarita. She is eighteen this night."

In the square patio the gentle breeze ruffled the pink and white oleander bushes. A long table set up on sawhorses held loaves of flaky crusted French bread, stacks of thin, delicate tortillas, plates of barbecued beef, and long red rolls of spicy sausages. But most of all there were cheeses, for the Three Marys was a cheese-eating valley. There were yellow cheese and white cheese and curded cheese from cows' milk. There was even a flat white cake of goat cheese from distant Linares, a delicacy too expensive for any but feast days.

To set off this feast were bottles of beer floating in ice-filled tin tubs, and another table was covered with bottles of mescal, of tequila, of maguey wine.

Don Roméo Calderón thrust a glass of tequila into the stranger's hand. "Drink, friend, to the prettiest girl in San Juan. As pretty as my fine fighting cocks, she is. On her wedding day she takes to her man, and by the Blessed Ribs may she find him soon, the best fighter in my flock. Drink deep, friend. Even the rivers flow with wine."

The Hidalgo man laughed and raised his glass high. "May the earth be always fertile beneath her feet."

Someone called to Don Roméo that more guests were arriving, and with a final delighted pat on the stranger's shoulder, the little man scurried away. As the young fellow smiled after his retreating host, his eyes caught and held another pair of eyes—laughing black eyes set in a young girl's face. The last time he had seen that face, it had been white and tense with rage, and the lips clenched tight to prevent an outgushing stream of angry words. That had been in February, and she had worn a white lace shawl over her hair. Now it was May, and a gardenia was a splash of white in the glossy dark braids. The moonlight had mottled his face that February night, and he knew that she did not recognize him. He grinned impudently back at her, and her eyes widened, then slid sideways to one of the chaperones. The fan in her small hand snapped shut. She tapped its parchment tip against her mouth and slipped away to join the dancing couples in the front room. The gestures of a fan translate into a coded language on the frontier. The stranger raised one eyebrow as he interpreted the signal.

But he did not move towards her at once. Instead, he inched slowly back against the table. No one was behind him, and his hands quickly unfastened the package he had been guarding so long. Then he nonchalantly walked into the front room.

The girl was sitting close to a chaperone. As he came up to her, he swerved slightly toward the bushy-browed old lady.

"Your servant, señora. I kiss your hands and feet."

The chaperone stared at him in astonishment. Such fine manners were not common to the town of San Juan Iglesias.

"Eh, you're a stranger," she said. "I thought so."

"But a stranger no longer, señora, now that I have met you." He bent over her, so close she could smell the faint fragrance of talcum on his freshly shaven cheek. "Will you dance the *parada* with me?"

This request startled her eyes into popping open beneath the heavy brows. "So, my young rooster, would you flirt with me, and I old enough to be your grandmother?"

"Can you show me a prettier woman to flirt with in the Valley of the Three Marys?" he asked audaciously.

She grinned at him and turned toward the girl at her side. "This young fool wants to meet you, my child."

The girl blushed to the roots of her hair and shyly lowered her white lids. The old woman laughed aloud.

"Go out and dance, the two of you. A man clever enough to pat the sheep has a right to play with the lamb."

The next moment they had joined the circle of dancers, and Sarita was trying to control her laughter.

"She is the worst dragon in San Juan. And how easily you won her!"

"What is a dragon," he asked imperiously, "when I longed to

dance with you?"

"*Ay,*" she retorted, "you have a quick tongue. I think you are a dangerous man."

In answer he drew her closer to him and turned her towards the orchestra. As he reached the chief violinist, he called out, "Play the 'Virgencita,' 'The Shy Young Maiden.' "

The violinist's mouth opened in soundless surprise. The girl in his arms said sharply, "You heard him, the 'Borachita,' 'The Little Drunken Girl.' "

With a relieved grin, the violinist tapped his music stand with his bow, and the music swung into the sad farewell of a man to his sweetheart:

"Farewell, my little drunken one,
I must go to the capital
To serve the master
Who makes me weep for my return."

The stranger frowned down at her. "Is this a joke, señorita?" he asked coldly.

"No," she whispered, looking about her quickly to see if the incident had been observed. "But the 'Virgencita' is the favorite song of Hidalgo, a village on the other side of the mountains in the next valley. The people of Hidalgo and San Juan Iglesias do not speak."

"That is a stupid thing," said the man from Hidalgo as he swung her around in a large turn. "Is not music free as air? Why should one town own the rights to a song?"

The girl shuddered slightly. "Those people from Hidalgo—they are wicked monsters. Can you guess what they did not six months since?"

The man started to point out that the space of time from February to May was three months, but he thought it better not to appear too wise. "Did these Hidalgo monsters frighten you, señorita? If they did, I personally will kill them all."

She moved closer against him and tilted her face until her mouth was close to his ear. "They attempted to steal the bones of Don Rómolo Balderas."

"Is it possible?" He made his eyes grow round and his lips purse up in disdain. "Surely not that! Why, all the world knows that Don Rómolo Balderas was the greatest historian in the entire Republic. Every school child reads his books. Wise men from Quintana Roo to the Río Bravo bow their heads in admiration to his name. What a wicked thing to do!" He hoped his virtuous tone was not too virtuous for plausibility, but she did not seem to notice.

"It is true! In the night they came. Three devils!"

"Young devils, I hope."

"Young or old, who cares? They were devils. The blacksmith surprised them even as they were opening the grave. He raised such a shout that all of San Juan rushed to his aid, for they were fighting, I can tell you. Especially one of them—their leader."

"And who was he?"

"You have heard of him, doubtless. A proper wild one named Pepe Gonzalez."

"And what happened to them?"

"They had horses and got away, but one, I think, was hurt."

The Hidalgo man twisted his mouth remembering how Rubén the candymaker had ridden across the whitewashed line high on the cañon trail that marked the division between the Three Marys' and the Sabinas' sides of the mountains, and then had fallen in a faint from his saddle because his left arm was broken. There was no candy in Hidalgo for six weeks, and the entire Sabinas Valley resented that broken arm as fiercely as did Rubén.

The stranger tightened his arm in reflexed anger about Sarita's waist as she said, "All the world knows that the men of Hidalgo are sons of the mountain witches."

"But even devils are shy of disturbing the honored dead," he said gravely.

" 'Don Rómolo was born in our village,' Hidalgo says. 'His bones belong to us.' Well, anyone in the valley can tell you he died in San Juan Iglesias, and here his bones will stay! Is that not proper? Is that not right?"

To keep from answering, he guided her through an intricate dance pattern that led them past the patio door. Over her head he could see two men and a woman staring with amazement at the open package on the table.

His eyes on the patio, he asked blandly, "You say the leader was one Pepe Gonzalez? The name seems to have a familar sound."

"But naturally. He has a talent." She tossed her head and stepped away from him as the music stopped. It was a dance of two *paradas*. He slipped his hand through her arm and guided her into place in the large oval of parading couples. Twice around the room and the orchestra would play again.

"A talent?" he prompted.

"For doing the impossible. When all the world says a thing cannot be done, he does it to prove the world wrong. Why, he climbed to the top of the Prow, and not even the long-vanished Joaquín Castillo had ever climbed that mountain before. And this same Pepe caught a mountain lion with nothing to aid him but a rope and his two bare hands."

"He doesn't sound such a bad friend," protested the stranger, slipping his arm around her waist as the music began to play the merry song of the soap bubbles:

> "Pretty bubbles of a thousand colors
> That ride on the wind
> And break as swiftly
> As a lover's heart."

The events in the patio were claiming his attention. Little by little he edged her closer to the door. The group at the table had considerably enlarged. There was a low murmur of excitement from the crowd.

"What has happened?" asked Sarita, attracted by the noise.

"There seems to be something wrong at the table," he answered, while trying to peer over the heads of the people in front of him. Realizing that this might be the last moment of peace he would have that evening, he bent toward her.

"If I come back on Sunday, will you walk around the plaza with me?"

She was startled into exclaiming, "*Ay*, no!"

"Please. Just once around."

"And you think I'd walk more than once with you, señor, even if you were no stranger? In San Juan Iglesias, to walk around the plaza with a girl means a wedding."

"Ha, and you think that is common to San Juan alone? Even the devils of Hidalgo respect that law." He added hastily at her puzzled upward glance, "And so they do in all the villages." To cover his lapse he said softly, "I don't even know your name."

A mischievous grin crinkled the corners of her eyes. "Nor do I know yours, señor. Strangers do not often walk the streets of San Juan."

Before he could answer, the chattering in the patio swelled to louder proportions. Don Roméo's voice lay on top, like thick cream on milk. "I tell you it is a jewel of a cheese. Such flavor, such texture, such whiteness. It is a jewel of a cheese."

"What has happened?" Sarita asked of a woman at her elbow.

"A fine goat's cheese appeared as if by magic on the table. No one knows where it came from."

"Probably an extra one from Linares," snorted a fat bald man on the right.

"Linares never made such a cheese as this," said the woman decisively.

"Silence!" roared Don Roméo. "Old Tío Daniel would speak a word to us."

A great hand of silence closed down over the mouths of the people. The girl was standing on tiptoe trying vainly to see what was happening. She was hardly aware of the stranger's whispering voice, although she remembered the words that he said. "Sunday night—once around the plaza."

She did not realize that he had moved away, leaving a gap that was quickly filled by the blacksmith.

Old Tío Daniel's voice was a shrill squeak, and his thin, stringy neck jutted forth from his body like a turtle's from its shell. "This is no cheese from Linares," he said with authority, his mouth sucking in over his toothless gums between his sentences. "Years ago, when the great Don Rómolo Balderas was still alive, we had such cheese as this—*ay*, in those days we had it. But after he died and was buried in our own sainted ground, as was right and proper. . . ."

"Yes, yes," muttered voices in the crowd. He glared at the interruption. As soon as there was silence again, he continued, "After he died, we had it no more. Shall I tell you why?"

"Tell us, Tío Daniel," said the voices humbly.

"Because it is made in Hidalgo!"

The sound of a waterfall, the sound of a wind in a narrow cañon, and the sound of an angry crowd are much the same. There were no distinct words, but the sound was enough.

"Are you certain, Tío?" boomed Don Roméo.

"As certain as I am that a donkey has long ears. The people of Hidalgo have been famous for generations for making cheese like this—especially that wicked one, that owner of a cheese factory, Timotéo Gonzalez, father to Pepe, the wild one, whom we have good cause to remember."

"We do, we do," came the sigh of assurance.

"But on the whole northern frontier there are no vats like his to produce so fine a product. Ask the people of Chihuahua, of Sonora. Ask the man on the bridge at Laredo, or the man in his boat at Tampico, '*Hola*, friend, who makes the finest goat cheese?' And the answer will always be the same, 'Don Timotéo of Hidalgo.' "

It was the blacksmith who asked the great question. "Then where did that cheese come from, and we haters of Hidalgo these ten long years?"

No voice said, "The stranger," but with one fluid movement every head in the patio turned toward the girl in the doorway. She also turned, her eyes wide with something that she realized to her own amazement was more apprehension than anger.

But the stranger was not in the room. When the angry, muttering men pushed through to the street, the stranger was not on the plaza. He was not anywhere in sight. A few of the more religious crossed themselves for fear that the devil had walked in their midst. "Who was he?" one voice asked another. But Sarita, who was meekly listening to a lecture from Don Roméo on the propriety of dancing with strangers, did not have to ask. She had a strong suspicion that she had danced that night within the circling arm of Pepe Gonzalez.

FOR DISCUSSION

1. An old rivalry exists between the citizens of Hidalgo and those of San Juan Iglesias. Are we told about its origin? Does the author treat this feud seriously? How do the people of Hidalgo and San Juan Iglesias seem to feel about it?

2. Compare this feud with any you know about in American history or literature.

Sunday Costs Five Pesos

A Comedy of Mexican Village Life

Cast (in order of appearance)

FIDEL
BERTA
SALOMÉ
TONIA
CELESTINA

THE TIME

The present. Early one Sunday afternoon.

THE SCENE

A housed-in square in the town called the Four Cornstalks (Las Cuatro Milpas) *in the northern part of Mexico. On the left of the square is the house of* TONIA, *with a door and a stoop. At the back is a wall cut neatly in half. The left side is the house of* BERTA *and boasts not only a door but a barred window. On the right is a square arch from which dangles an iron lantern. This is the only exit to the rest of the town, for on the right side proper is the house of* SALOMÉ. TONIA'S *house is pink, and* SALOMÉ'S *is blue, while* BERTA'S *is content with being a sort of disappointed yellow. All three houses get their water from the well that is down center left.*

It is early afternoon on Sunday, and all sensible people are sleeping, but through the arch comes FIDEL DURÁN. *His straw hat in his hand, his hair plastered to his head with water, he thinks he is a very handsome sight indeed as he pauses, takes a small mirror from his pocket, fixes his neck bandanna . . . a beautiful purple one with orange spots, and shyly knocks, then turns around with a broad grin on his face.*

BERTA *opens the door.* BERTA *is very pretty, but unfortunately she has a very high temper, possibly the result of her red hair.*

She wears a neat cotton dress and tennis shoes, blue ones. Her hands fastened on her hips, she stands and glares at FIDEL.

BERTA. Oh, so it is you!

FIDEL (*beaming on her*). A good afternoon to you, Berta.

BERTA (*sniffing*). A good afternoon indeed, and I bothered by fools at this hour of the day.

FIDEL (*in amazement*). Why Berta, are you angry with me?

BERTA (*questioning heaven*). He asks me if I am angry with him. Saints in heaven, has he no memory?

FIDEL (*puzzled*). What have I done, Berta?

BERTA (*sarcastically*). Nothing, Fidel, nothing. That is the trouble. But if you come to this house again, I will show you the palm of my hand, as I'm showing it to you now. (*She slaps him, steps inside the door, and slams it shut.*)

FIDEL (*pounding on the door*). Open the door, Berta. Open the door! I must speak to you!

[*The door of* SALOMÉ'S *house opens, and* SALOMÉ *herself comes out with a small pitcher and begins drawing water from the well. She is twenty-eight, and so many years of hunting a husband have left her with an acid tongue.*]

SALOMÉ. And this is supposed to be a quiet street.

FIDEL (*who dislikes her*). You tend to your affairs, Salomé, and I will tend to mine. (*He starts pounding again. He bleats like a young goat hunting for its mother.*) Berta, Berta.

BERTA (*opens the door again*). I will not have such noises. Do you not realize that this is Sunday afternoon? Have you no thoughts for decent people who are trying to sleep?

FIDEL. Have you no thoughts for me?

BERTA. More than one. And none of them nice.

SALOMÉ. I would call this a lovers' quarrel.

BERTA. Would you indeed! (*Glares at* FIDEL.) I would call it the impertinence of a wicked man!

FIDEL (*helplessly*). But what have I done?

SALOMÉ. She loved him yesterday, and she will love him tomorrow.

BERTA (*runs down to* SALOMÉ). If I love him tomorrow, may I lose the use of my tongue, yes, and my eyes and ears too.

FIDEL (*swinging* BERTA *to one side*). Is it fair, I ask you, for a woman to smile at a man one day and slap his face the next? Is this the manner in which a promised bride should treat her future husband?

SALOMÉ (*grins and winks at him*). You could find yourself another bride.

BERTA (*angrily*). We do not need your advice, Salomé Molina. You and your long nose . . . sticking it in everyone's business.

SALOMÉ (*her eyes flashing*). Is this an insult to me? To me?

BERTA. And who are you to be above insults?

SALOMÉ. I will not stay and listen to such words!

BERTA. Did I ask you to leave the safety of your home?

SALOMÉ (*to* FIDEL). She has not even common politeness. I am going!

BERTA. We shall adore your absence.

SALOMÉ. If this were not Sunday, I would slap your face for you.

BERTA (*taunting*). The great Salomé Molina, afraid of a Sunday fine.

FIDEL (*wanting to be helpful*). You can fight each other tomorrow. There is no fine for weekdays.

SALOMÉ. You stay out of this argument, Fidel Durán.

FIDEL. If you do not leave us, I will never find out why Berta is angry with me. (*Jumps toward her.*) Go away!

SALOMÉ (*jumps back, then tosses her head*). Very well. But the day will come when you will be glad of my company. (*She goes indignantly into her house.*)

FIDEL (*turns to* BERTA). Now, Berta.

BERTA (*interrupting*). As for you, my fine rooster, go and play the bear to Celestina García. She will appreciate you more than I.

FIDEL (*with a guilty hand to his mouth*). So that is what it is.

BERTA (*on the stoop of her own house*). That is all of it, and enough it is. Two times you walked around the plaza with the Celestina last night, and I sitting there on a bench having to watch you. (*Goes into the house.*)

FIDEL (*speaking through the open door*). But it was a matter of business.

BERTA (*enters with a broom and begins to sweep off the stoop*). Hah! Give me no such phrases. And all of my friends thinking, "Poor Berta, with such a sweetheart." Do you think I have no pride?

FIDEL. But it is that you do not understand. . . .

BERTA. I understand enough to know that all is over between us.

FIDEL. Berta, do not say that. I love you.

BERTA. So you say. And yet you roll the eye at any passing chicken.

FIDEL. Celestina is the daughter of Don Nimfo García.

BERTA. She can be the daughter of the president for all of me. When you marry her, she will bring you a fine dowry, and there will be no more need of Fidel Durán trying to carve wooden doors.

FIDEL (*his pride wounded*). Trying? But I have carved them. Did I not do a new pair for the saloon?

BERTA. Aye, little doors . . . doors that amount to no more than that. . . . (*She snaps her fingers.*) Not for you the great doors of a church.

FIDEL. Why else do you think I was speaking with the Celestina?

BERTA (*stops sweeping*). What new manner of excuse is this?

FIDEL. That is why I came to speak with you. Sit down here on the step with me for a moment.

BERTA (*scandalized*). And have Salomé and Tonia say that I am a wicked, improper girl?

FIDEL (*measuring a tiny space between his fingers*). Just for one little moment. They will see nothing.

BERTA (*sitting down*). Let the words tumble out of your mouth, one, two, three.

FIDEL. Perhaps you do not know that the town of Topo Grande, not thirty kilometers from here, is building a new church.

BERTA (*sniffs*). All the world knows that.

FIDEL. But did you know that Don Nimfo is secretly giving the money for the building of that church?

BERTA. Why?

FIDEL. He offered the money to the Blessed Virgin of Topo Grande if his rooster won in the cockfight. It did win, so now he is building the church.

BERTA (*not yet convinced*). How did you find out about this? Or has Don Nimfo suddenly looked upon you as a son and revealed all his secrets to you?

FIDEL. Last night on the plaza the Celestina happened to mention it. With a bit of flattery I soon gained the whole story from her.

BERTA. So that is what you were talking about as you walked around the plaza? (*Stands.*) It must have taken a great deal of flattery to gain so much knowledge from her.

FIDEL (*stands*). Do you not realize what it means? They will need someone to carve the new doors.

[*He strikes a pleased attitude, expecting her to say, "But how wonderful, Fidel."*]

BERTA (*knowing very well what* FIDEL *expects, promptly turns away from him, her hand hiding a smile, as she says with innocent curiosity*) I wonder whom Don Nimfo will get? (*With the delight of discovery.*) Perhaps the Brothers Ochóa from Monterrey.

FIDEL (*crestfallen*). He might choose me.

BERTA. You? Hah!

FIDEL. And why not? Am I not the best woodcarver in the valley?

BERTA. So you say.

FIDEL. It would take three years to carve those doors, and he would pay me every week. There would be enough to buy you a trousseau and enough left over for a house.

BERTA. Did you tell all that to the Celestina?

FIDEL. Of course not! Does a girl help a man buy a trousseau for another girl? That was why it had to appear as though I were rolling the eye at her. (*He is very much pleased with his brilliance.*)

BERTA. Your success was more than perfect. Today all the world knows that the Celestina has won Berta's man.

FIDEL. But all the world does not know that Fidel Durán, who is I, myself, will carve those doors so as to buy a trousseau and house for Berta, my queen.

BERTA. Precisely. All the world does not know this great thing. . . . (*Flaring out at him.*) And neither do I!

FIDEL. Do you doubt me, pearl of my life?

BERTA. Does the rabbit doubt the snake? Does the tree doubt the lightning? Do I doubt that you are a teller of tremendous lies? Speak not to me of cleverness. I know what my own eyes see, and I saw you flirting with the Celestina. Last night I saw you . . . and so did all the world!

FIDEL (*beginning to grow angry*). So that is how you trust me, your intended husband.

BERTA. I would rather trust a hungry fox.

FIDEL. Let me speak plainly, my little dove. Because we are to be married is no reason for me to enter a monastery.

BERTA. And who says that we are to be married?

FIDEL (*taken aback*). Why . . . I said it.

BERTA. Am I a dog to your heel that I must obey your every wish?

FIDEL (*firmly*). You are my future wife.

BERTA (*laughs loudly*). Am I indeed?

FIDEL. Your mother has consented, and my father has spoken. The banns have been read in the church! (*Folds his arms with satisfaction.*)

BERTA (*screaming*). Better to die without children than to be married to such as you.

FIDEL (*screaming above her*). We shall be married within the month.

BERTA. May this hand rot on my arm if I ever sign the marriage contract.

FIDEL. Are you saying that you will not marry me?

BERTA. With all my mouth I am saying it, and a good day to you. (*Steps inside the house and slams the door. Immediately opens it and sticks her head out.*) Tell that good news to that four-nosed shrew of a Celestina. (*Slams the door again.*)

[FIDEL *puts on his hat and starts toward the archway, then runs down and pounds on* TONIA'S *door, then runs across and pounds on* SALOMÉ'S. *In a moment both girls come out.* TONIA *is younger and smaller in size than either* SALOMÉ *or* BERTA *and has a distressing habit of whining.*]

SALOMÉ. What is the meaning of this noise?

TONIA. Is something wrong?

FIDEL. I call you both to witness what I say. May I drop dead if I am ever seen in this street again!

[*He settles his hat more firmly on his head, and with as much dignity as he can muster, he strides out through the arch. The girls stare after him, then at* BERTA'S *door, then at each other. Both shrug; then with one accord they run up and begin knocking on the door.*]

SALOMÉ. Berta!

TONIA. Berta, come out!

[BERTA *enters. She is obviously trying to keep from crying.*]

SALOMÉ. Has that fool of a sweetheart of yours lost his mind?

TONIA. What happened?

BERTA (*crying in earnest*). This day is blacker than a crow's wing. Oh, Salomé!

[*She flings both arms about the girl's neck and begins to wail loudly.* TONIA *and* SALOMÉ *stare at each other, and then* TONIA *pats* BERTA *on the shoulder.*]

TONIA. Did you quarrel with Fidel?

SALOMÉ. Of course she quarreled with him. Any fool could see that.

BERTA. He will never come back to me. Never!

TONIA (*to* SALOMÉ). Did she say anything about the Celestina to him?

SALOMÉ (*to* BERTA). You should have kept your mouth shut on the outside of your teeth.

BERTA. A girl has her pride, and no Celestina is going to take any man of mine.

TONIA. But did she take him?

BERTA (*angrily to* TONIA). You take your face away from here!

SALOMÉ. The only thing you can do now is to ask him to come back to you.

TONIA (*starting toward the archway*). I will go and get him.

BERTA (*clutches at her*). I will wither on my legs before I ask him to come back. He would never let me forget that I had to beg him to marry me. (*Wails again.*) And now he will marry the Celestina. (TONIA *begins to cry with her.*)

TONIA. There are other men.

BERTA. My heart is with Fidel. My life is ruined.

SALOMÉ (*thoughtfully*). If we could bring him back without his knowing Berta had sent for him. . . . (*She sits on the edge of the well.*)

TONIA. Miracles only happen in the church.

SALOMÉ (*catches her knee and begins to rock back and forth*). What could we tell him? What could we tell him?

TONIA. You be careful, Salomé, or you will fall in the well. Then we will all have to go into mourning, and Berta can not get married at all if she is in mourning.

SALOMÉ (*snaps her fingers*). You could fall down the well, Berta! That would bring him back.

BERTA (*firmly*). I will not fall down the well and drown for any man, not even Fidel.

TONIA. What good would bringing him back do if Berta were dead?

SALOMÉ. Now that is a difficulty. (*Begins to pace up and down.*) If you are dead, you cannot marry Fidel. If you are not dead, he will not come back. The only thing left for you is to die an old maid.

TONIA. That would be terrible.

BERTA (*wailing*). My life is ruined. Completely ruined.

SALOMÉ (*with sudden determination*). Why? Why should it be?

TONIA (*with awe*). Salomé has had a thought.

BERTA. You do not know what a terrible thing it is to lose the man you love.

SALOMÉ. I am fixing up your life, not mine. Suppose . . . suppose you did fall in the well.

BERTA. I tell you I will not do it.

SALOMÉ. Not really, but suppose he thought you did. What then?

BERTA. You mean . . . pretend? But that is a sin! The priest would give me ten days' penance at confession.

SALOMÉ (*flinging out her hands*). Ten days' penance or a life without a husband. Which do you choose?

TONIA. I will tell you. She chooses the husband. What do we do, Salomé?

SALOMÉ. You run and find this carver of doors. Tell him that a great scandal has happened . . . that Berta has fallen in the well.

TONIA (*whose dramatic imagination has begun to work*). Because she could not live without him. . . .

BERTA. You tell him that and I will scratch out both your eyes!

TONIA. On Sunday?

BERTA (*sullenly*). On any day.

SALOMÉ. Tell him that Berta has fallen in the well and that you think she is dying.

TONIA. Is that all?

BERTA. Is that not enough?

SALOMÉ (*entranced with the idea*). Oh, it will be a great scene, with Berta so pale in her bed, and Fidel kneeling in tears beside it.

BERTA. I want you to know that I am a modest girl.

SALOMÉ (*irritated*). You can lie down on the floor, then. (*Glaring at* TONIA.) What are you standing there for? Run!

TONIA (*starts toward the archway, then comes back*). But . . . where will I go?

SALOMÉ. To the place where all men go with a broken heart . . . the saloon. Are you going to stand there all day?

[TONIA *gives a little gasp and runs out through the arch.*]

BERTA. I do not like this idea. If Fidel finds out it is a trick, he will be angrier than ever.

SALOMÉ. But if he does not find out the truth until after you are married . . . what difference will it make?

BERTA. He might beat me.

SALOMÉ. Leave that worry until after you are married. (*Inspecting* BERTA.) Now, how will we make you look pale? Have you any flour? Corn meal might do.

BERTA. No! No! I will not do it.

SALOMÉ. Now, Berta, be reasonable.

BERTA. If I had really fallen down the well, it would be different. But I did not fall down it.

SALOMÉ. Do you not want Fidel to come back to you? Are you in love with him?

BERTA. Yes, I do love him. And I will play no tricks on him. If he loves the Celestina better than he does me . . . (*with great generosity*) he can marry her.

SALOMÉ (*pleading with such idiocy*). But Tonia has gone down to get him. If he comes back and finds you alive . . . he will be angrier than ever.

BERTA (*firmly*). This is your idea. You can get out of it the best way you can. But Fidel will not see me lying down on a bed, nor on a floor, nor anyplace else.

SALOMÉ. Then there is only one thing to do.

BERTA. What is that?

SALOMÉ. You will go into the house, and I will tell him that you are too sick to see him.

BERTA. That will be just as bad as the other.

SALOMÉ. How can it be? Then if he finds out it is a trick, he will blame me, and you can pretend you knew nothing of it. I do not care how angry he is. I do not want to marry him.

BERTA (*with pleased excitement*). Then he could not be angry with me, could he? I mean if he thought I had nothing to do with it? And I would not have to do penance either, would I?

SALOMÉ. Not one day of penance. Tonia should have found him by now. (*Goes to the arch and peers through.*) Here they come . . . and Fidel is running half a block in front of her.

BERTA (*joyously*). Then he does love me!

SALOMÉ. Into the house with you. You can watch through the window.

BERTA (*on stoop*). Now, remember, if he gets angry, this was your idea.

SALOMÉ (*claps her hands*). And what a beautiful idea it is!

[BERTA *disappears into the house.* SALOMÉ *looks about her, then dashes over to her own stoop, sits down, flings her shawl over her face, and begins to moan loudly, rocking back and forth. In a moment* FIDEL *dashes through the arch and stops, out of breath, at seeing* SALOMÉ.]

FIDEL (*gasping*). Berta!

SALOMÉ (*whose moaning grows louder*). Poor darling, poor darling. She was so young.

FIDEL (*desperately*). She is . . . she is dead?

SALOMÉ (*wailing*). She will make such a beautiful corpse. Poor darling. Poor darling.

[TONIA, *exhausted and out of breath, has reached the arch.*]

TONIA (*looks about her in astonishment*). Why, where is Berta? Did she go into the house?

SALOMÉ (*in normal tones*). Of course she went into the house, you fool. Did she not jump down the well? (*Remembering* FIDEL.) Poor darling.

TONIA (*blankly*). Did she really jump down it? I thought she just fell in by accident.

SALOMÉ (*grimly*). Are you telling this story . . . or am I? (*Wailing.*) Now she can never go to the plaza again.

[FIDEL *looks helplessly from* TONIA, *who cannot quite get the details of the story straight, to* SALOMÉ, *who is having a beautiful time mourning.*]

FIDEL. Where is she? I want to see her.

TONIA (*coming out of her trance*). She is right in here. Did you say she was on the bed or on the floor, Salomé?

SALOMÉ (*getting between them and* BERTA'S *door*). You don't want to see her, Fidel. You know how people look after they've been drowned.

TONIA. But he was supposed to see her. That was why you sen. . . .

SALOMÉ (*glaring at her*). Tonia, dear, suppose that you let me tell the story. After all, I was here and you were not.

FIDEL (*exploding*). For the love of the saints, tell me! Is she dead?

SALOMÉ (*thinking this over*). Well . . . not exactly.

FIDEL. You mean . . . you mean there is hope?

SALOMÉ. I would say there was great hope.

FIDEL (*takes off his hat and mops his face*). What can I do? Oh, if I could only see her. . . .

SALOMÉ. If you would go to the church and light a candle to Our Blessed Lady and ask her to forgive you for getting angry with Berta . . . perhaps things will arrange themselves.

FIDEL. Do you think she will get well soon?

SALOMÉ. With a speed that will amaze you.

FIDEL. I will go down and light the candle right now.

[*As he turns to leave, who should come through the archway but* CELESTINA GARCÍA. *She can match temper for temper with* BERTA *any day, and right now she is on the warpath. Brushing past these three as though they did not exist, she goes up to* BERTA'S *door and pounds on it.*]

CELESTINA. I dare you to come out and call this Celestina García a four-nosed shrew to her face.

SALOMÉ (*trying to push* FIDEL *through the arch*). You had best run to the church.

FIDEL (*pushing past her and going up to* CELESTINA). How dare you speak like that to a poor drowned soul?

SALOMÉ (*to* CELESTINA). Why do you not go away? We never needed you so little.

CELESTINA. So she is pretending to be drowned, eh? Is that her coward's excuse?

BERTA (*through window*). Who dares to call Berta Cantú a coward?

CELESTINA. You know well enough who calls you, and I the daughter of Don Nimfo García.

TONIA. *Ay,* Salomé! And now Fidel will know that Berta was not drowned at all.

FIDEL (*who has been listening to this conversation with growing surprise and suspicion, now turns furiously toward* BERTA'S *house*). Not drowned, eh? So this was a trick to bring me back, eh? I am through with your tricks, you hear me? Through with them!

BERTA (*through window*). You stay right there until I come out. (*She disappears from view.*)

FIDEL (*turning to* SALOMÉ). I see your hand in this.

SALOMÉ. The more fool you to be taken in by a woman's tricks.

CELESTINA. What care I for tricks? No woman is going to call me names!

BERTA (*coming through the door*). You keep silence, Celestina García. I will deal with you in a minute. And as for you, Fidel Durán. . . .

FIDEL (*stormily*). As for me, I am finished with all women. The world will see me no more. I will enter a monastery and carve as many doors as I like. Do you hear me, Berta Cantú?

BERTA (*putting both hands over her ears*). What do I care for your quack, quack, quack!

FIDEL. Now she calls me a duck! Good afternoon to you! (*He stalks out with wounded dignity.*)

CELESTINA (*catching* BERTA *by the shoulder and swinging her around*). I ask you again; did you call me a four-nosed shrew?

BERTA. I did, and I will repeat it with the greatest of pleasure. You are a four-nosed shrew and a three-eyed frog!

CELESTINA. I have always looked on you as my friend . . . you pink-toed cat!

BERTA. And I have always trusted you . . . you sly robber of bridegrooms!

[*She raises her hand to slap* CELESTINA. SALOMÉ *catches it.*]

SALOMÉ. This is Sunday, Berta! And Sunday costs five pesos.

TONIA. If you had to pay a fine for starting a fight on top of losing Fidel. . . . *Ay,* that would be terrible.

[BERTA *and* CELESTINA *glare at each other, and then slowly begin to circle each other, spitting out their insults as they do so.*]

CELESTINA. It is my honor that is making me fight, or I would wait until tomorrow.

BERTA. If I had five pesos to throw away, I would pull out your dangling tongue . . . leaving only the flapping roots.

CELESTINA. Ha! I make a nose at your words.

BERTA. As for you . . . you eater of ugly-smelling cheese. . . .

[*They jump at each other, but remember the penalty just in time and pull back. Again they begin to circle around, contenting themselves with making faces at each other.* SALOMÉ *suddenly clasps her hands.*]

SALOMÉ. You are both certain that you want to fight today?

CELESTINA. Why else do you think I came here?

BERTA. These insults have gone too far to stop now.

SALOMÉ. The only thing that stands in the way is the five pesos for the Sunday fine.

TONIA. And five pesos is a lot of money.

SALOMÉ. Then the only thing to do is to play the fingers.

CELESTINA. What?

BERTA. Eh?

SALOMÉ. Precisely. Whoever loses strikes the first blow and pays the fine. Then you can fight as much as you like.

TONIA (*with awed admiration*). *Ay,* Salomé, you have so many brains.

CELESTINA (*doubtfully*). It is a big risk.

BERTA (*shrugging*). Perhaps you are afraid of taking a risk.

CELESTINA. I am not afraid of anything. But Tonia will have to be the judge. Salomé is too clever.

BERTA. Very well. But Salomé has to stand behind you to see that you do not cheat. I would not trust you any more than I would a mouse near a piece of fresh bacon.

CELESTINA (*pulls back her clenched fist, then thinks better of it, and speaks with poor grace*). Very well.

[CELESTINA *and* BERTA *stand facing each other.* TONIA *stands between them up on the stoop.* SALOMÉ *stands behind* CELESTINA.]

TONIA (*feeling a little nervous over this great honor of judging*). Both arms behind your backs. (*The girls link their arms behind them.*) Now, when I drop my hand, Berta will guess first as

Celestina brings her fingers forward. The first girl to guess correctly twice wins. Are you ready? (*All nod.*) I am going to drop my arm.

SALOMÉ. Celestina, put out your fingers before Berta guesses. We will have no cheating.

CELESTINA (*sullenly*). Very well.

[*She puts out two fingers behind her, and* SALOMÉ, *seeing this, raises up her arm with two fingers extended, opening and closing them scissors fashion.* BERTA *frowns a little as she looks up at the signal, and* CELESTINA, *seeing this, swings around and looks at* SALOMÉ, *who promptly grins warmly and pretends to be waving at* BERTA. CELESTINA *then looks at* TONIA.]

BERTA. Very well.

CELESTINA (*guessing as* BERTA *swings her arm forward*). Three.

[BERTA *triumphantly holds up one finger. Biting her lip,* CELESTINA *starts to swing forward her own arm.* SALOMÉ, *intent on signaling* BERTA, *holds up her own five fingers spread wide and does not notice until too late that* CELESTINA *has swung around to watch her.*]

CELESTINA (*screaming*). So I cheat, eh?

[*With that she gives* SALOMÉ *a resounding slap on the cheek. The next moment the two women are mixed up in a beautiful howling, grunting fight, while* TONIA *and* BERTA, *wide-eyed, cling together and give the two women as much space as possible. Let it be understood that this is only a fight of kicking, hair-pulling, and scratching. There is no man involved, nor a point of honor. Rather a matter of angry pride. So the two are not attempting to mutilate each other. They are simply gaining satisfaction. The grand finale comes when* CELESTINA *knocks* SALOMÉ *to the ground and sits on her.*]

CELESTINA (*breathing hard*). There! That was worth five pesos.

TONIA. You have to pay it. And Don Nimfo will be angry with you.

CELESTINA (*pulling herself to her feet*). I am too tired to fight any more now, but I will be back next Tuesday, Berta, and then I will beat you up.

BERTA (*sniffing*). If you can.

CELESTINA (*warningly*). And there is no fine on Tuesday.
BERTA. Come any day you like. I will be ready for you.
TONIA (*to* CELESTINA). You should be ashamed to fight.
CELESTINA. Who are you to talk to me? (*Stamps her foot at* TONIA, *who jumps behind* BERTA.) Good afternoon, my brave little rabbits!

[*She staggers out as straight as she can, but as she reaches the archway, she feels a twinge of agony and is forced to limp. By this time* SALOMÉ *has gathered together what strength she has left, and she slowly stands up. Once erect, she looks at* BERTA *and* TONIA *as though she were considering boiling in oil too good for them.*]

SALOMÉ (*with repressed fury*). My friends. My very good friends.
TONIA (*frightened*). Now, Salomé. . . .
SALOMÉ (*screaming*). Do not speak to me! Either of you! (*She manages to get to the door of her house.*) When I need help, do you give me aid? No! But just you wait . . . both of you!
TONIA. What are you going to do?
SALOMÉ. I am going to wait for a weekday, and then I am going to beat up both of you at once. One (*she takes a deep breath*) with each hand! (*She nearly falls through the door of her house.*)
BERTA (*with false bravado*). Who is afraid of her?
TONIA. I am. Salomé is very strong. It is all your fault. If you had not gotten mad at Fidel, this would not have happened.
BERTA (*snapping at her*). You leave Fidel out of this.
TONIA (*beginning to cry*). When Salomé beats me up, that will be your fault too.
BERTA. Stop crying!
TONIA. I am not a good fighter, but I can tell Fidel the truth about how you would not jump down the well to win him back.
BERTA. You open your mouth to Fidel and I will push you in the well.
TONIA. You will not have strength enough to push a baby in the well when they get through with you.
BERTA. Get out! Get out of here!

[*She stamps her foot at* TONIA, *and the girl, frightened, gives a squeak and runs into her own house.* BERTA *looks after her; then, beginning to sniffle, she goes over and sits on the well. She acts like a child who has been told that it is not proper for little girls to cry, and she is very much in need of a handkerchief. Just then* FIDEL *sticks his head around the arch.*]

FIDEL (*once more the plaintive goat*). Berta.

[BERTA *half jumps, then pretends not to hear him.*]

FIDEL (*enters cautiously, not taking his eyes off* BERTA'S *stiff back. He moves around at the back, skirts* TONIA'S *house, then works his way round to her.*). Berta.
BERTA (*sniffing*). What is it?
FIDEL (*circling the back of the well*). Are you crying, Berta?
BERTA (*stubbornly*). No!
FIDEL (*sitting beside her*). Yes, you are. I can see you crying.
BERTA. If you can see, why do you ask, then?
FIDEL. I am sorry we quarreled, Berta.
BERTA. Are you?
FIDEL. Are you sorry?
BERTA. No!
FIDEL. I was hoping you were, because . . . do you know whom I saw on the plaza?
BERTA. Grandfather Devil.
FIDEL. Don Nimfo himself.
BERTA. Perhaps you saw the Celestina, too.
FIDEL (*placatingly*). Now, Berta, you know I do not care if I never see the Celestina again. (*Pulls out a handkerchief and extends it to her.*) Here, wipe your face with this.
BERTA. I have a handkerchief of my own. (*Nevertheless, she takes it and wipes her eyes and then blows her nose.*)
FIDEL. Don Nimfo said I could carve the church doors for him. But he said I would have to move to Topo Grande to work on them. He said I had to leave right away.
BERTA (*perking up her interest*). You mean . . . move away from here?
FIDEL. And I was wondering if we could get married tomorrow. I know this is very sudden, Berta, but after all, think how long I have waited to carve a church door.

BERTA. Tomorrow. (*She looks toward* SALOMÉ'S *house.*) They would both be too sore to do anything by tomorrow.

FIDEL (*too concerned with his own plans to hear what she is saying*). Of course I know that you may not be able to forgive me....

BERTA. Fidel, I want you to understand that if I do marry you tomorrow ... that means we will leave here tomorrow, eh?

FIDEL. *Ay,* yes. I have to be in Topo Grande on Tuesday.

BERTA. I hope you will always understand what a great thing I have done for you. It is not every girl who would forgive so easily as I.

FIDEL (*humbly*). Indeed, I know that, Berta.

BERTA. Are you quite sure that we will leave here tomorrow?

FIDEL. Quite sure.

BERTA. Very well. I will marry you.

FIDEL (*joyfully*). Berta! (*Bends forward to kiss her. She jumps up.*)

BERTA. Just a moment. We are not married yet. Do you think that I am just any girl that you can kiss me ... like that! (*She snaps her fingers.*)

FIDEL (*humbly*). I thought ... just this once....

BERTA (*gravely thoughtful*). Well, perhaps ... just this once ... you may kiss my hand.

As he kisses it,

The Curtains Close

FOR DISCUSSION

1. Do you think the characters in this play are realistically portrayed? Support your answers with examples of things said or done by the characters.

2. What do you think is the author's attitude toward her characters?

3. Of all the characters in "The Street of the Three Crosses," "The Engagement," "The Street of the Cañon," and *Sunday Costs Five Pesos,* which did you like best? Describe the traits you most admired. Which did you like least? Why?

Rafael Jesús González

b. 1935

Rafael Jesús González spent his boyhood in El Paso, Texas. He attended the University of Texas at El Paso, where he was president of the student literary society. González also studied at the National University of Mexico and now teaches English at Laney College in Oakland, California.

"To an Old Woman" was written while González was still a student. The poem indicates the position of love and influence held by the mother in Mexican-American families.

To an Old Woman

Come, mother—
   Your rebozo trails a black web
   And your hem catches on your heels.
You lean the burden of your years
On shaky cane, and palsied hand pushes
   Sweat-grimed pennies on the counter.
Can you still see, old woman,
The darting color-trailed needle of your trade?
   The flowers you embroider
   With three-for-a-dime threads
Cannot fade as quickly as the leaves of time.

What things do you remember?
Your mouth seems to be forever tasting
The residue of nectar-hearted years.
Where are the sons you bore?
Do they speak only English now
And pass for Spaniards?
Did California lure them
To forget the name of *madre?*
One day I know you will not come
And ask for me to pick
The colors you can no longer see.
I know I'll wait in vain
For your toothless benediction.
I'll look into the dusty street
Made cool by pigeons' wings
Until a dirty child will nudge me and say:
"Señor, how much ees thees?"

FOR DISCUSSION

What is the significance of the last two lines of the poem?

Mario Suarez

b. 1925

Mario Suarez has been writing since his college days at the University of Arizona, where he was greatly helped and encouraged by his teacher Ruth Keenan, and where he also studied under the late Richard Summers and folklorist Frances Cilmore. In 1957 he received a John Hay Whitney Foundation Fellowship for creative writing. At present he is on the faculty of Chicano Studies at California State Polytechnic College in Pomona.

A "city boy" who grew up in Tucson, Arizona, he writes about his childhood neighborhood; his stories tell of the colorful characters in the barrio, *where life styles have a quality all their own.*

"El Hoyo," a general description of the Tucson barrio, *sets the scene for several selections about characters living there. Señor Garza, in the story of the same title, tries to reach a happy medium between work and pleasure. In "Maestria" Gonzalo Pereda fears that the times have passed him by. As you read these selections, notice the difference between the urban way of life described by Suarez and the country style depicted by Josephina Niggli.*

El Hoyo

From the center of downtown Tucson the ground slopes gently away to Main Street, drops a few feet, and then rolls to the banks of the Santa Cruz River. Here lies the sprawling section of the city known as El Hoyo. Why it is called El Hoyo is not clear.

It is not a hole as its name would imply; it is simply the river's immediate valley. Its inhabitants are Chicanos who raise hell on Saturday night, listen to Padre Estanislao on Sunday morning, and then raise more hell on Sunday night. While the term *Chicano* is the short way of saying *Mexicano,* it is the long way of referring to everybody. Pablo Gutierrez married the Chinese grocer's daughter and acquired a store; his sons are Chicanos. So are the sons of Killer Jones who threw a fight in Harlem and fled to El Hoyo to marry Cristina Mendez. And so are all of them—the assortment of harlequins,[1] bandits, oppressors, oppressed, gentlemen, and bums who came from Old Mexico to work for the Southern Pacific, pick cotton, clerk, labor, sing, and go on relief. It is doubtful that all of these spiritual sons of Mexico live in El Hoyo because they love each other—many fight and bicker constantly. It is doubtful that the Chicanos live in El Hoyo because of its scenic beauty—it is everything but beautiful. Its houses are built of unplastered adobe, wood, license plates, and abandoned car parts. Its narrow streets are mostly clearings which have, in time, acquired names. Except for the tall trees which nobody has ever cared to identify, nurse, or destroy, the main things known to grow in the general area are weeds, garbage piles, dogs, and kids. And it is doubtful that the Chicanos live in El Hoyo because it is safe—many times the Santa Cruz River has risen and inundated the area.

In other respects, living in El Hoyo has its advantages. If one is born with the habit of acquiring bills, El Hoyo is where the bill collectors are less likely to find you. If one has acquired the habit of listening to Señor Perea's Mexican Hour in the wee hours of the morning with the radio on at full blast, El Hoyo is where you are less likely to be reported to the authorities. Besides, Perea is very popular, and to everybody sooner or later is dedicated "The Mexican Hat Dance." If one has inherited a bad taste for work but inherited also the habit of eating, where, if not in El Hoyo, are the neighbors more willing to lend you a cup of flour or beans? When Señora García's house burned to the ground with all her belongings and two kids, a benevolent gentleman conceived the gesture that put her on the road to solvency. He took five hundred names and solicited from each a dollar. At the end of the week

[1] HARLEQUINS: here, clowns; buffoons.

he turned over to the heartbroken but grateful señora three hundred and fifty dollars in cold cash and pocketed his recompense. When the new manager of a local business decided that no more Mexican girls were to work behind his counters, it was the Chicanos of El Hoyo who acted as pickets and, on taking their individually small but collectively great buying power elsewhere, drove the manager out, and the girls returned to their jobs. When the Mexican Army was enroute to Baja California and the Chicanos found out that the enlisted men ate only at infrequent intervals, they crusaded across town with pots of beans, trays of tortillas, boxes of candy, and bottles of wine to meet the train. When someone gets married, celebrating is not restricted to the immediate families and friends of the couple. The public is invited. Anything calls for a celebration, and in turn a celebration calls for anything. On Armistice Day[2] there are no fewer than half a dozen fights at the Tira-Chancla Dance Hall. On Mexican Independence Day more than one flag is sworn allegiance to and toasted with gallon after gallon of Tumba Yaqui.

And El Hoyo is something more. It is this something more which brought Felipe Ternero back from the wars after having killed a score of Germans, with his body resembling a patchwork quilt. It helped him to marry a fine girl named Julia. It brought Joe Zepeda back without a leg from Luzon[3] and helps him hold more liquor than most men can hold with two. It brought Jorge Casillas, a gunner flying B-24's over Germany, back to compose boleros. Perhaps El Hoyo is the proof that those people exist who, while not being against anything, have as yet failed to observe the more popular modes of human conduct. Perhaps the humble appearance of El Hoyo justifies the discerning shrugs of more than a few people only vaguely aware of its existence. Perhaps El Hoyo's simplicity motivates many a Chicano to move far away from its intoxicating *frenesi*, its dark narrow streets, and its shrieking children, to deny the blood-well from which he springs, to claim the blood of a conquistador[4] while his hair is straight and his face beardless. Yet

[2] Armistice Day: now called Veterans' Day.

[3] Luzon: one of the Philippine Islands, a battleground during World War II.

[4] conquistador (kŏn•kwĭs′tə•dôr): one of the Spanish conquerors of Mexico and Peru in the sixteenth century.

El Hoyo is not the desperate outpost of a few families against the world. It fights for no causes except those which soothe its immediate angers. It laughs and cries with the same amount of passion in times of plenty and of want.

Perhaps El Hoyo, its inhabitants, and its essence can best be explained by telling you a little bit about a dish called *capirotada.* Its origin is uncertain. But it is made of old, new, stale, and hard bread. It is sprinkled with water, and then it is cooked with raisins, olives, onions, tomatoes, peanuts, cheese, and general leftovers of that which is good and bad. It is seasoned with salt, sugar, pepper, and sometimes chili or tomato sauce. It is fired with tequila or sherry wine. It is served hot, cold, or just "on the weather," as they say in El Hoyo. The Garcías like it one way, the Quevedos another, the Trilos another, and the Ortegas still another. While in general appearance it does not differ much from one home to another, it tastes different everywhere. Nevertheless, it is still *capirotada.* And so it is with El Hoyo's Chicanos. While many seem to the undiscerning eye to be alike, it is only because collectively they are referred to as Chicanos. But like *capirotada,* fixed in a thousand ways and served on a thousand tables, which can only be evaluated by individual taste, the Chicanos must be so distinguished.

FOR DISCUSSION

Describe what the word *slum* means to you. Would you call El Hoyo a slum? Do you think neighborhoods such as El Hoyo should be cleared away, or preserved? Explain.

Señor Garza

Many consider Garza's Barber Shop as not truly in El Hoyo because it is on Congress Street and therefore downtown. Señor Garza, its proprietor, cashier, janitor, and Saint Francis, philosophizes that since it is situated in that part of the street where the land decidedly slopes, it is in El Hoyo. Who would question it? Who contributes to every cause for which a solicitor comes in with a long face and a longer relation of sadness? Who is the easiest touch for all the drunks who have to buy their daily cures? For loafers who go to look for jobs and never find them? For bullfighters on the wrong side of the border? For boxers still amateurs though punchy? For barbers without barber shops? And for the endless line of moochers who drop in to borrow anything from two bits to two dollars? Naturally, Garza.

Garza's Barber Shop is more than razors, scissors, and hair. It is where men, disgruntled at the vice of the rest of the world, come to air their views. It is where they come to get things off their chests along with the hair off their heads and beard off their faces. Garza's Barber Shop is where everybody sooner or later goes or should. This does not mean that there are no other barber shops in El Hoyo. There are. But none of them seem quite to capture the atmosphere that Garza's does. If it were not downtown, it would probably have a little fighting rooster tied to a stake by the front door. If it were not rented to Señor Garza only, it would perhaps smell of sherry wine all day. To Garza's Barber Shop goes all that is good and bad. The lawbreakers come in to rub elbows with the sheriff's deputies. And toward all Garza is the same. When zoot-suiters[1] come in for a very slight trim, Garza, who is very versatile, puts on a bit of zoot talk and hep-cats with the zootiest of them. When the boys that are not zoot-suiters come in, he becomes, for the purpose of accommodating his clientele, just as big a snob as their individual personalities require. When necessity

[1] ZOOT-SUITERS: Zoot suits were made of flashy material and had padded shoulders, long jackets, and full trousers tapered to narrow cuffs.

calls for a change in his character, Garza can assume the proportions of a Greek, a Chinaman, a gypsy, a republican, a democrat, or if only his close friends are in the shop, plain Garza.

Perhaps Garza's pet philosophy is that a man should not work too hard. Garza tries not to. His day begins according to the humor of his wife. When Garza drives up late, conditions are perhaps good. When Garza drives up early, all is perhaps not well. Garza's Barber Shop has been known, accordingly, to stay closed for a week. It has also been known to open before the sun comes up and to remain open for three consecutive days. But on normal days and with conditions so-so, Garza comes about eight in the morning. After opening, he pulls up the green venetian blinds. He brings out two green ash cans containing the hair cut the preceding day and puts them on the edge of the sidewalk. After this he goes to a little back room in the back of the shop, brings out a long crank, and lowers the red awning that keeps out the morning sun. Lily-boy, the fat barber who through time and diligence occupies chair number two, is usually late. This does not mean that Lily-boy is lazy, but he is married, and there are rumors, which he promptly denies, that state he is henpecked. Rodriguez, barber number three, usually fails to show up for five out of six workdays.

On ordinary mornings Garza sits in the shoeshine stand, because it is closest to the window, and nods at the pretty girls going to work and to the ugly ones, too. He works on an occasional customer. He goes to Sally and Sam's for a cup of coffee, and on returning continues to sit. At noon Garza takes off his small apron, folds it, hangs it on the arm of his chair, and after combing his hair goes to La Estrella to eat and flirt with the waitresses who, for reasons that even they cannot understand, have taken him into their confidence. They are well aware of his marital standing; but Garza has black wavy hair and a picaresque[2] charm that sends them to the kitchen giggling. After eating his usual meal of beans, rice, tortilla, and coffee, he bids all the girls good-bye and goes back to his barber shop. The afternoons are spent in much the same manner as the mornings, except that on such days as Saturday, there is such a rush of business that Garza very often seeks

[2] PICARESQUE: like a *picaro*, a clever rogue or vagabond adventurer.

some excuse to go away from his own business and goes for the afternoon to Nogales in Mexico or downstairs to the Tecolote Club to drink beer.

On most days, by five-thirty everybody has usually been in the shop for friendly reasons, commercial reasons, and even spiritual reasons. Loco-Chu, whose lack of brains everybody understands, has gone by and insulted the customers. Take-It-Easy, whose liquor-saturated brain everybody respects, has either made nasty signs at everybody or has come in to quote the words and poems of the immortal Antonio Plaza. Cuco has come from his job at Feldman's Furniture Store to converse of the beauty of Mexico and the comfort of the United States. Procuna has come in, and being a university student with more absences than the rest of his class put together, has very politely explained his need for two dollars until the check comes in. Chonito has shined shoes and danced a dozen or so boogie pieces. There have been arguments. Fortunes made and lost. Women loved. The great Cuate Cuete has come in to talk of the glory and grandeur of zoot-suitism in Los Angeles. Old customers due about that day have come. Also new ones who had to be told that all the loafers who seemingly live in Garza's Barber Shop were not waiting for haircuts. Then the venetian blinds are let down. The red awning is cranked up. The door is latched on the inside, although it is continually opened on request for friends, and the remaining customers are attended to and let out.

Inside, Garza opens his little National Cash Register, counts the day's money, and puts it away. He opens his small writing desk and adds and subtracts for a little while in his green record book. Meanwhile, Chonito grudgingly sweeps and says very nasty words. Lily-boy phones his wife to tell her that he is about to start home and that he will not be waylaid by friends and that he will not arrive drunk. Rodriguez relates to everybody in the shop that when he was a young man, getting tired was not like him. The friends who have already dropped in wait until the beer is spoken for, and then Chonito is sent for it. When it is brought in and distributed, everything is talked about. Lastly, women are thoroughly insulted, although their necessity is emphasized. Garza, being a man of experience and one known to say what he feels when he feels it, recalls the ditty he heard while still in the cradle and says, "To women neither all your love nor all your money." The friends, drinking Garza's beer, agree.

Not always has Señor Garza enjoyed the place of distinction if not of material achievement that he enjoys among his friends today. In his thirty-five years his life has gone through transition after transition, conquest after conquest, setback after setback. But now Señor Garza is one of those to whom most refer, whether for reasons of friendship, indebtedness, or of having never read Plato and Aristotle, as an oracle pouring out his worldly knowledge during and between the course of his haircuts.

Garza was born in El Hoyo, the second of seven Garzas. He was born with so much hair that perhaps this is what later prompted him to be a barber. At five he almost burned the house down while playing with matches. At ten he was still waiting for his older brother to outgrow his clothes so that they could be handed down to him. Garza had the desire to learn, but even before he found out about school, Garza had already attained a fair knowledge of everything. Especially the knowledge of want. Finally, his older brother got a new pair of overalls and Garza got his clothes. On going to school he immediately claimed having gone to school in Mexico, so Garza was tried out in the 3B. In the 4A his long legs fitted under the desk, so he had to begin his education there. In the 5B he fell in love with the teacher and was promptly promoted to avert a scandal. When Garza was sixteen and had managed to get to the eighth grade, school suddenly became a mass of equations, blocks, lines, angles, foreign names, and headaches. At seventeen it might have driven him to insanity, so Garza wisely cut his schooling short at sixteen.

On leaving school Garza tried various enterprises. He became a delivery boy for a drugstore. He became a stockroom clerk for a shoe store. But of all enterprises the one he found most profitable was that of shearing dogs. He advertised his business, and it flourished until it became very obvious that his house and brothers were getting quite flea-ridden. Garza had to give it up. The following year he was overcome with the tales of vast riches in California. Not that there was gold, but there were grapes to be picked. He went to California. But of that trip he has more than once said that the tallness of the California garbage cans made him come back twenty pounds lighter and without hair under his armpits.

Garza then tried the CCC[3] camp. But it turned out that there were too many bosses with muscles that looked like golf balls whom Garza thought it best not to have much to do with. Garza was already one that could keep everybody laughing all day long, but this prevented almost everybody from working. At night when most boys at camp were either listening to the juke box in the canteen or listening to the playing of sad guitars, Garza trimmed heads at fifteen cents. After three months of piling rocks, carrying logs, and of getting fed up with his bosses' perpetual desires of making him work, Garza came back to the city with the money he had saved cutting hair, and through a series of deals was allowed a barber's chair in a going establishment.

In a few years Garza came to be a barber of prominence. He had grown to love the idle conversation that is typical of barber shops, the mere idle gossip that often speaks of broken homes and forsaken women in need of friends. These Garza has always sought and in his way has done his best to put in higher spirits. Even after his marriage he continued to receive anonymous after anonymous phone call. He came to know the bigtime operators and their brand of filthy doings. He came to know the bootleggers, thieves, and rustlers. He came to know also the smalltime operators with the bigtime complex and their shallowness of human understanding. He came to know false friends that came to him and said, "We're throwing a dance. We've got a good crowd. The tickets are two dollars." And on feeling superior, once the two dollars had fattened their wallets and inflated their conceit, remarked upon seeing him at the dance, "Damn, even the barber came." But in time Garza has seen many of these grow fat. He has seen their women go unfaithful. He has seen them get spiritually lost in trying to keep up materially with the people next door. He has seen them go bankrupt buying gabardine to make up for their lack of style. Their hair had cooties but smelled of aqua-rosa. The edges of their underwear were frilled, even though they wore new suits. They gave breakfasts for half of the city to prove that "they had" and only ended up with piles of dirty dishes. Garza watched, philosophized, cut more hair, and of this has more than once said in the course of a beer or idle conversation among friends,

[3] CCC: Civilian Conservation Corps, a government agency which hired unemployed young men for public conservation work in the 1930s.

"Damned fools, when you go, how in the hell are you going to take it with you? You are buried in your socks. Your suit is slit in the back and placed on top of you."

So in time Garza became the owner of his own barber shop. Garza's Barber Shop with its three Koken barber chairs, its reception sofas, its shoeshine stand, washbowls, glass kits, pictures, objects to be sold and raffled, and juke box. Second to none in its colorful array of true friends and false, of drunks, loafers, bullfighters, boxers, other barbers, moochers, and occasional customers. Perfumed with the poetry of the immortal Antonio Plaza, and seasoned with naughty jokes told at random.

Soon the night becomes old, and empty beer bottles are collected and put in the little back room. Chonito, who has swept the floor while Garza and his friends have consumed beer, asks for a fifty-cent advance or swears with the power of his fourteen years that he will never sweep the shop again, and gets it. Lily-boy phones his wife again and tells her that he is about to start home and that he is sober. Rodriguez, if he worked that day, says he has a bad cold which he must go home to cure, but asks for an advance to buy his tonic at Tom's Liquor Store. Then the lights are switched off, and Garza, his barbers, his friends, and Chonito file out. Garza, not forgetting the words he heard while in the cradle, "To women neither all your love nor all your money," either goes up the street to the Royal Inn for a glass of beer or to the All States Pool Hall. Then he goes home. Garza, a philosopher. Owner of Garza's Barber Shop. But the shop will never own Garza.

FOR DISCUSSION

1. Is Garza a good businessman? Use examples from the story to support your argument. Describe his attitude toward work. How does his attitude compare with what you believe is the typical American attitude toward work?

2. Señor Garza has *machismo:* he is his own boss; he speaks his mind freely; he is quite popular with the ladies. One of his favorite expressions is "To women neither all your love nor all your money." Discuss your opinion of *machismo.*

Maestria

Whenever a man is referred to as a *maestro,* it means that he is master of whatever trade, art, or folly he practices. If he is a shoemaker, for example, he can design, cut, and finish any kind of shoe he is asked for. If he is a musician, he knows composition, direction, execution, and thereby plays Viennese waltzes as well as the bolero. If he is a thief, he steals thousands, for he would not damn his soul by taking dimes. That is *maestria.* It is applied with equal honor to a painter, tailor, barber, printer, carpenter, mechanic, bricklayer, window washer, ditchdigger, or bootblack if his ability merits it. Of course, when a man is graying and has no apparent trade or usefulness, out of courtesy people may forget he is a loafer and will call him a *maestro.* Whether he is or not is of no importance. Calling him a *maestro* hurts no one.

During the hard times of Mexico's last revolution[1] many *maestros* left Mexico with their families with the idea of temporarily making a living north of the Rio Grande. But the revolution lasted for such a long time that when it finally came to an end, the *maestros,* now with larger families, remained here in spite of it. During the hard times of the last depression they opened little establishments on West Broad Street and North Pike where they miraculously made a dollar on some days and as many as two or three on others—always putting on, because they were used to hard times, a good face. When good times returned, most of the *maestros* closed up their little establishments and went to work for the larger concerns which came back in business. Some left for the increasing number of factory jobs in California. But some, enjoying their long independence and believing that it is better to be a poor lord than a rich servant, kept their little establishments open.

Gonzalo Pereda, for example, was a *maestro* who kept a little saddle shop open on West Broad Street. Being a great conversationalist, he was not against having company at all hours. Being easy with his money, he was always prey for those that told him of need in their homes. And easier prey still for those that often

[1] MEXICO'S LAST REVOLUTION: In 1910, the dictator Porfirio Díaz was ousted and a more democratic government established. The revolution lasted for seven years.

talked him into closing up his establishment so that they might gossip of old times over a bottle of beer. Being a good craftsman, therefore, had never helped to give the *maestro* more than enough with which to provide for his family.

But if there were men in the world who worried about their work after being through for the day, as far as the *maestro* was concerned, they deserved to die young. It certainly was not so with Gonzalo Pereda. Life, he figured, was too short anyway. When he closed up in the afternoon, he rid his mind completely of jobs pending and overhead unpaid. He simply hurried home to feed his stable of fighting roosters and to eat supper with his family. Even before taking off his hat he made his way to the back yard to see that his roosters had fresh water and that their cages were clean. That the *maestro* did all of this before going to greet his family does not mean that he liked the roosters better. But the family, now grown up and with its own affairs, could wait. The roosters, dependent on his arrival for their care, could and should not.

One day when the *maestro* came home, he found a little cage in his back yard. Attached to the top of it was a tag which read, "A present from your friend Bernabe Lerda. Chihuahua, Mexico." In the cage was a red rooster. The *maestro* stuck his finger through an opening and had to jerk it out immediately when the rooster picked at it with a bill which seemed to be made of steel. The *maestro* took a thin leather strip from his pocket, opened the cage, and tied it to the rooster's leg. Then he took the rooster out in order to examine him carefully. The *maestro* looked closely at the rooster's long thick legs, at his tail, which by its length might have belonged to a peacock, at the murder in both of his eager eyes; and the *maestro* knew that this rooster would assassinate any unfortunate fowl pitted against him.

After gazing around a bit the little rooster stretched and strutted. He flapped his wings a few times, and then he crowed. The *maestro* was amazed. How could it be, he asked himself, that an animal could possess such pomp? How was it that he knew he was a better rooster than any other that had ever emerged from a hen's egg and therefore strutted about like a racehorse confident of winning the Kentucky Derby? How did he know he was such a handsome example of chickenhood that he, without doubt, could be the Valentino of any chicken yard? Well, it was unbelievable, but it was so. And the *maestro* was sure that this rooster, being from Mexico, no less, would slash his way to thirty victories once they put him in the pit. A few minutes later, when one of the *maestro*'s sons saw the rooster, both decided that he must have a worthy name: they decided to call him *Killer*.

So great a stir did Killer cause that the *maestro* forgot all about eating supper that night. While he watched admiringly, Killer took his time about eating his grain and drinking his cool water. One would have thought that the *maestro* could aliment[2] himself by merely gazing at the conceited rooster as he strutted about. The *maestro* said, "The minute he goes into the pit, the other rooster will drop dead from fright. Just look at the beautiful creature."

And so it was. The following Sunday afternoon the *maestro* burst in through the front door with Killer. Killer was still hot under the wings from having chased the other rooster and then having slashed it to ribbons. He was still kicking inside the cage as if asking for all the roosters who ever sported a gaff[3] to take him on. "You should have seen him," said the *maestro* to his wife. "Killer is the greatest rooster that ever lived." Then he took Killer to the back yard to cool off.

During the night there was a big commotion in the yard. Killer had gotten out of his cage and was attacking the other roosters through the wire fronts of their cages. Already, in a minute or so, there was blood in front of the cage belonging to a rooster named General, who had retreated to the back of his cage for safety. Killer was squaring off, with his neck feathers ruffled, at another cage, in an effort to pick out the eyes of a rooster named Diablo. "He is really cute, isn't he?" asked the *maestro*. Then he took Killer, and holding him said, "Well, I guess it is only natural for him to want to fight. He had no competition this afternoon." When Killer was put in another cage, the *maestro* and his son went back to bed.

After the Killer's second fight, the following Sunday, the *maestro* once again came in through the front door with Killer. This time

[2] ALIMENT: supply with food; nourish.

[3] GAFF: metal spur attached to the leg of a gamecock during a cockfight.

Killer had disposed of his adversary in less than two minutes. The *maestro* was happy. "I am convinced," he said, "that Killer is a butcher if there ever was one." And in victory the *maestro* brought Killer through the front door after the third, fourth, and fifth fights. Now, of course, Killer traveled to and from the pit in style. His was a big cage, made and designed to give him a lot of comfort, with letters reading "Killer."

On the Sunday that Killer won his sixth fight, the *maestro* was so happy when he brought Killer through the front door for his wife to admire that tears came from his eyes as he said, "Every rooster that sees this champion can say that the devil has taken him." And on that day Killer established himself firmly as the best rooster that had ever come to fall into the *maestro's* possession. This Sunday, after all, had been a great one for the *maestro,* financially speaking and otherwise.

The following Sunday the *maestro* got up very early. Before his daughter left for church, he had her take out the camera in order to photograph Killer. The picture that came out best would be sent away to *Hook and Gaff,* a magazine dedicated to cockfights and poultry. They photographed Killer from various angles. In the arms of the *maestro.* Perched on top of a pole. Looking into a hen roost.

But that afternoon, after the fight, the *maestro* did not storm through the front door to tell how Killer had all but peeled and removed the entrails from the opposing rooster. The *maestro* hurried around the side of the house to the back yard with Killer in his hands. Killer, the invincible one, had met his match. After six battles had come his Waterloo. The reason that Killer was not dead was because the *maestro* had stopped the fight and forfeited his bet. But Killer seemed more dead than alive. His bill was open as if to force breath into his lungs. One of his wings was almost torn off. His back was deeply gashed. One of his eyes was closed. The *maestro* worked frantically to keep Killer alive. He put flour under the torn wing. He took a damp rag and wiped the blood off Killer's head. The *maestro* looked as though he had lost his best friend.

For many days the Killer did not eat. He only stood, and weakly, on his long, thick legs. The *maestro* came home many times to take care of him. He brought Killer some baby-chicken feed in order that he might eat something when he recuperated enough to open his eyes. But to no avail. The *maestro*'s gladiator still seemed close to death.

Then, of a sudden, Killer got better. He began to pick at the baby-chicken feed. And the *maestro* was overwhelmed with joy. Killer did not strut as before, or crow, or flap his wings; but he would, in time. Many things, the *maestro* often said, were fixed by time alone.

Towards the end of Killer's convalescence the *maestro* felt proud of the job he had done in rescuing the Killer from death. As a finishing touch he decided to give the rooster, who was beginning to act somewhat like the Killer of old, some little pieces of liver. These would give him more blood. So while the *maestro*'s son opened Killer's bill, the *maestro* pushed a little piece of liver down Killer's throat. But the second piece caused Killer to gurgle, to kick momentarily, and then suddenly to die in the *maestro*'s hands. With tears in his eyes the *maestro* stroked his beloved Killer, bit his lip as he wrapped the limp body of his Spartan in a newspaper, and tenderly put it in the garbage can. Then, without supper, the *maestro* went to bed. His beloved Killer was gone.

Like Killer's plight, it might be added, is the plight of many things the *maestros* cherish. Each year they hear their sons talk English with a rapidly disappearing accent, that accent which one early accustomed only to Spanish never fails to have. Each year the *maestros* notice that their sons' Spanish loses fluency. But perhaps it is natural. The *maestros* themselves seem to forget about bulls and bullfighters, about guitars and other things so much a part of the world that years ago circumstances forced them to leave behind. They hear instead more about the difference between one baseball swing and another. Yes, perhaps it is only natural.

Ofttimes when *maestros* get together, they point out the fact that each year there are less and less of their little establishments around. They proudly say that the old generation was best; that the new generation knows nothing. They point out, for example, that there are no shoemakers any more. They say that the new generation of so-called shoemakers are nothing but repairers of cheap shoes in need of half soles. They say that the musicians are but accompanists who learned to play an instrument in ten lessons and thus take money under false pretenses. Even the thieves, they tell you, are nothing but two-bit clips. The less said about other phases of *maestria,* they will add, the better.

When one of the *maestros* dies, all the other *maestros* can be counted upon to mourn him. They dust off the dark suits they seldom wear, and offer him, with their calloused hands folded in prayer, a rosary or two. They carry his coffin to and from the church. And they help fill his grave with the earth that will cover him thereafter. Then they silently know the reason why there are not so many of the little establishments as before. Perhaps it is natural. There are not so many *maestros* any more.

FOR DISCUSSION

1. What qualities does Gonzalo exhibit which win him the respect of others and earn him the title *maestro?*

2. Killer's death is an event of much more importance than merely the death of a fighting rooster. What does it signify?

3. Would you be inclined to agree with the *maestros'* evaluation of the younger generation?

Luís Omar Salinas

b. 1937

Born in Robstown, Texas, Luís Omar Salinas lived in Mexico for several years, then with his uncle and aunt in Bakersfield, California. After graduation from a local high school, he attended various California colleges, working his way through as a dishwasher, construction worker, and newspaper reporter.

In this poem Salinas pays tribute to the great Mexican singer Pedro Infante, whose songs may still be heard in Mexican cantinas and on Spanish-language radio stations throughout the Southwest. (Notice once again that Mexican-American culture is truly international, drawing its aspects from both sides of the Rio Grande.)

Pedro

(*Pedro Infante—Mexican Singer, Actor,*
Genius, who died piloting his own
plane, April, 1957, at the age of
thirty-seven)

You took the world and embraced
  it as a child
    your arms
        your voice
            your heart
  touched the sea

you had many loves
among them Mexico

when you died
it rose to its feet
to pay homage to you

mountains of snow
were singing
your songs

Pedro I remember you
when I was a child
and how you brought
tears

silence within silence

FOR DISCUSSION

1. Why did the speaker in the poem admire Pedro Infante?
2. What does the poet mean by his phrase "silence within silence"?

Amado Muro

b. 1931

Amado Muro was born in Parral, Chihuahua, where his father was a singer and composer of ballads. At an early age he moved to El Paso, Texas, and attended school there. He has worked as a field hand and a construction worker, and he has traveled to Europe and South America as a seaman. When not traveling, he lives and works in El Paso.

Like Suarez, Muro describes life in the barrio. *Among the inhabitants of the* barrio *Muro finds singers, musicians, poets, and philosophers. Life is certainly not dreary here. Still, there are problems, such as the pain of adolescent love described in this story.*

Cecilia Rosas

When I was in the ninth grade at Bowie High School in El Paso, I got a job hanging up women's coats at La Feria Department Store on Saturdays. It wasn't the kind of job that had much appeal for a Mexican boy or for boys of any other nationality, either. But the work wasn't hard, only boring. Wearing a smock, I stood around the Ladies' Wear Department all day long waiting for women customers to finish trying on coats so I could hang them up.

Having to wear a smock was worse than the work itself. It was an agonizing ordeal. To me it was a loathsome stigma of unmanly toil that made an already degrading job even more so. The work itself I looked on as onerous[1] and effeminate for a boy from a family of miners, shepherds, and ditchdiggers. But working in Ladies'

[1] ONEROUS (ŏn′ər•əs): burdensome; oppressive.

Wear had two compensations: earning three dollars every Saturday was one; being close to the Señorita Cecilia Rosas was the other.

This alluring young woman, the most beautiful I had ever seen, more than made up for my mollycoddle labor and the smock that symbolized it. My chances of looking at her were almost limitless. And like a good Mexican, I made the most of them. But I was only too painfully aware that I wasn't the only one who thought this saleslady gorgeous.

La Feria had water fountains on every one of its eight floors. But men liked best the one on the floor where Miss Rosas worked. So they made special trips to Ladies' Wear all day long to drink water and look at her.

Since I was only fourteen and in love for the first time, I looked at her more chastely than most. The way her romantic lashes fringed her obsidian[2] eyes was especially enthralling to me. Then, too, I never tired of admiring her shining raven hair, her Cupid's-bow lips, the warmth of her gleaming white smile. Her rich olive skin was almost as dark as mine. Sometimes she wore a San Juan rose in her hair. When she did, she looked so very lovely I forgot all about what La Feria was paying me to do and stood gaping at her instead. My admiration was decorous but complete. I admired her hourglass figure as well as her wonderfully radiant face.

Other men admired her too. They inspected her from the water fountain. Some stared at her boldly, watching her trimly rhythmic hips sway. Others, less frank and open, gazed furtively at her swelling bosom or her shapely calves. Their effrontery made me indignant. I, too, looked at these details of Miss Rosas. But I prided myself on doing so more romantically, far more poetically, than they did, with much more love than desire.

Then, too, Miss Rosas was the friendliest as well as the most beautiful saleslady in Ladies' Wear. But the other salesladies, Mexican girls all, didn't like her. She was so nice to them all they were hard put to justify their dislike. They couldn't very well admit they disliked her because she was pretty. So they all said she was haughty and imperious. Their claim was partly true. Her beauty was Miss Rosas' only obvious vanity. But she had still another. She

[2] OBSIDIAN: Obsidian is a lustrous volcanic glass, usually black.

prided herself on being more American than Mexican because she was born in El Paso. And she did her best to act, dress, and talk the way Americans do. She hated to speak Spanish, disliked her Mexican name. She called herself Cecile Roses instead of Cecilia Rosas. This made the other salesladies smile derisively. They called her La Americana or the Gringa from Xochimilco every time they mentioned her name.

Looking at this beautiful girl was more important than money to me. It was my greatest compensation for doing work that I hated. She was so lovely that a glance at her sweetly expressive face was enough to make me forget my shame at wearing a smock and my dislike for my job with its eternal waiting around.

Miss Rosas was an exemplary saleslady. She could be frivolous, serious, or demure, primly efficient too, molding herself to each customer's personality. Her voice matched her exotically mysterious eyes. It was the richest, the softest, I had ever heard. Her husky whisper, gentle as a rain breeze, was like a tender caress. Hearing it made me want to dream, and I did. Romantic thoughts burgeoned up in my mind like rosy billows of hope scented with Miss Rosas' perfume. These thoughts made me so languid at my work that the floor manager, Joe Apple, warned me to show some enthusiasm for it or else suffer the consequences.

But my dreams sapped my will to struggle, making me oblivious to admonitions. I had neither the desire nor the energy to respond to Joe Apple's warnings. Looking at Miss Rosas used up so much of my energy that I had little left for my work. Miss Rosas was twenty, much too old for me, everyone said. But what everyone said didn't matter. So I soldiered on the job and watched her, entranced by her beauty, her grace. While I watched, I dreamed of being a hero. It hurt me to have her see me doing such menial work. But there was no escape from it. I needed the job to stay in school. So more and more I took refuge in dreams.

When I had watched her as much, if not more, than I could safely do without attracting the attention of other alert Mexican salesladies, I slipped out of Ladies' Wear and walked up the stairs to the top floor. There I sat on a window ledge smoking Faro cigarettes, looking down at the city's canyons, and best of all, thinking about Miss Rosas and myself.

They say Chihuahua Mexicans are good at dreaming because the mountains are so gigantic and the horizons so vast in Mexico's biggest state that men don't think pygmy thoughts there. I was no exception. Lolling on the ledge, I became what I wanted to be. And what I wanted to be was a handsome American Miss Rosas could love and marry. The dreams I dreamed were imaginative masterpieces, or so I thought. They transcended the insipid realities of a casual relationship, making it vibrantly thrilling and infinitely more romantic. They transformed me from a colorless Mexican boy who put women's coats away into the debonair American, handsome, dashing, and worldly, that I longed to be for her sake. For the first time in my life I reveled in the magic of fantasy. It brought happiness. Reality didn't.

But my window-ledge reveries left me bewildered and shaken. They had a narcotic quality. The more thrillingly romantic fantasies I created, the more I needed to create. It got so I couldn't get enough dreaming time in Ladies' Wear. My kind of dreaming demanded disciplined concentration. And there was just too much hubbub, too much gossiping, too many coats to be put away there.

So I spent less time in Ladies' Wear. My flights to the window ledge became more recklessly frequent. Sometimes I got tired sitting there. When I did, I took the freight elevator down to the street floor and brazenly walked out of the store without so much as punching a time clock. Walking the streets quickened my imagination, gave form and color to my thoughts. It made my brain glow with impossible hopes that seemed incredibly easy to realize. So absorbed was I in thoughts of Miss Rosas and myself that I bumped into Americans, apologizing mechanically in Spanish instead of English, and wandered down South El Paso Street like a somnambulist,[3] without really seeing its street vendors, cafés and arcades, tattoo shops, and shooting galleries at all.

But if there was confusion in these walks, there was some serenity too. Something good did come from the dreams that prompted them. I found I could tramp the streets with a newly won tranquility, no longer troubled by, or even aware of, girls in tight skirts, overflowing blouses, and drop-stitch stockings. My love for Miss Rosas was my shield against the furtive thoughts and indiscriminate

[3] SOMNAMBULIST (sŏm•năm′byə•ləst): sleepwalker.

desires that had made me so uneasy for a year or more before I met her.

Then, too, because of her, I no longer looked at the pictures of voluptuous women in the *Vea* and *Vodevil* magazines at Zamora's newsstand. The piquant thoughts Mexicans call *malos deseos* were gone from my mind. I no longer thought about women as I did before I fell in love with Miss Rosas. Instead, I thought about a woman, only one. This clear-cut objective and the serenity that went with it made me understand something of one of the nicest things about love.

I treasured the walks, the window-ledge sittings, and the dreams that I had then. I clung to them just as long as I could. Drab realities closed in on me chokingly just as soon as I gave them up. My future was a time clock with an American Mister telling me what to do, and this I knew only too well. A career as an ice-dock laborer stretched ahead of me. Better said, it dangled over me like a Veracruz machete. My uncle, Rodolfo Avitia, a straw boss[4] on the ice docks, was already training me for it. Every night he took me to the mile-long docks overhanging the Southern Pacific freight yards. There he handed me tongs and made me practice tripping three-hundred-pound ice blocks so I could learn how to unload an entire boxcar of ice blocks myself.

Thinking of this bleak future drove me back into my fantasies, made me want to prolong them forever. My imagination was taxed to the breaking point by the heavy strain I put on it.

I thought about every word Miss Rosas had ever said to me, making myself believe she looked at me with unmistakable tenderness when she said them. When she said, "Amado, please hang up this fur coat," I found special meaning in her tone. It was as though she had said, "Amadito, I love you."

When she gave these orders, I pushed into action like a man blazing with a desire to perform epically heroic feats. At such times I felt capable of putting away not one but a thousand fur coats, and would have done so joyously.

Sometimes on the street I caught myself murmuring, "Cecilia, *linda amorcita*, I love you." When these surges swept over me, I walked down empty streets so I could whisper, "Cecilia, *te quiero*

[4] STRAW BOSS: worker who acts as boss or assistant foreman in addition to his regular duties.

con toda mi alma"[5] as much as I wanted to and mumble everything else that I felt. And so I emptied my heart on the streets and window ledge while women's coats piled up in Ladies' Wear.

But my absences didn't go unnoticed. Once an executive-looking man, portly, gray, and efficiently brusque, confronted me while I sat on the window ledge with a Faro cigarette pasted to my lips, a cloud of tobacco smoke hanging over my head, and many perfumed dreams inside it. He had a no-nonsense approach that jibed with his austere mien. He asked me what my name was, jotted down my work number, and went off to make a report on what he called "sordid malingering."

Other reports followed his. Gruff warnings, stern admonitions, and blustery tirades developed from them. They came from both major and minor executives. These I was already inured to. They didn't matter anyway. My condition was far too advanced, already much too complex, to be cleared up by mere lectures, fatherly or otherwise. All the threats and rebukes in the world couldn't have made me give up my window-ledge reveries or kept me from roaming city streets with Cecilia Rosas' name on my lips like a prayer.

The reports merely made me more cunning, more doggedly determined to city-slick La Feria out of work hours I owed it. The net result was that I timed my absences more precisely and contrived better lies to explain them. Sometimes I went to the men's room and looked at myself in the mirror for as long as ten minutes at a time. Such self-studies filled me with gloom. The mirror reflected an ordinary Mexican face, more homely than comely. Only my hair gave me hope. It was thick and wavy, deserving a better face to go with it. So I did the best I could with what I had, and combed it over my temples in ringlets just like the poets back in my hometown of Parral, Chihuahua, used to do.

My inefficiency, my dreams, my general lassitude, could have gone on indefinitely, it seemed. My life at the store wavered between bright hope and leaden despair, unrelieved by Miss Rosas' acceptance or rejection of me. Then one day something happened that almost made my overstrained heart stop beating.

It happened on the day Miss Rosas stood behind me while I put a fur coat away. Her heady perfume, the fragrance of her warm

[5] *te . . . alma:* I love you with all my soul.

healthy body, made me feel faint. She was so close to me I thought about putting my hands around her lissome waist and hugging her as hard as I could. But thoughts of subsequent disgrace deterred me, so instead of hugging her I smiled wanly and asked her in Spanish how she was feeling.

"Amado, speak English," she told me. "And pronounce the words slowly and carefully, so you won't sound like a country Mexican."

Then she looked at me in a way that made me the happiest employee who ever punched La Feria's time clock.

"Amadito," she whispered the way I had always dreamed she would.

"Yes, Señorita Cecilia," I said expectantly.

Her smile was warmly intimate. "Amadito, when are you going to take me to the movies?" she asked.

Other salesladies watched us, all smiling. They made me so nervous I couldn't answer.

"Amadito, you haven't answered me," Miss Rosas said teasingly. "Either you're bashful as a village sweetheart, or else you don't like me at all."

In voluble Spanish, I quickly assured her the latter wasn't the case. I was just getting ready to say, "Señorita Cecilia, I more than like you; I love you" when she frowned and told me to speak English. So I slowed down and tried to smooth out my ruffled thoughts.

"Señorita Cecilia," I said. "I'd love to take you to the movies any time."

Miss Rosas smiled and patted my cheek. "Will you buy me candy and popcorn?" she said.

I nodded, putting my hand against the imprint her warm palm had left on my face.

"And hold my hand?"

I said "yes" so enthusiastically it made her laugh. Other salesladies laughed too. Dazed and numb with happiness, I watched Miss Rosas walk away. How proud and confident she was, how wholesomely clean and feminine. Other salesladies were looking at me and laughing.

Miss Sandoval came over to me. *"Ay papacito,"* she said. "With women you're the divine tortilla."

Miss de la Rosa came over too. "When you take the Americana

to the movies, remember not to speak Christian," she said. "And be sure you wear the pants that don't have any patches on them."

What they said made me blush and wonder how they knew what we had been talking about. Miss Arroyo came over to join them. So did Miss Torres.

"Amado, remember women are weak and men aren't made of sweet bread," Miss Arroyo said.

This embarrassed me, but it wasn't altogether unpleasant. Miss Sandoval winked at Miss de la Rosa, then looked back at me.

"Don't go too fast with the Americana, Amado," she said. "Remember the procession is long and the candles are small."

They laughed and slapped me on the back. They all wanted to know when I was going to take Miss Rosas to the movies. "She didn't say," I blurted out without thinking.

This brought another burst of laughter. It drove me back up to the window ledge, where I got out my package of Faros and thought about the wonderful thing that had happened. But I was too nervous to stay there. So I went to the men's room and looked at myself in the mirror again, wondering why Miss Rosas liked me so well. The mirror made it brutally clear that my looks hadn't influenced her. So it must have been something else, perhaps character. But that didn't seem likely either. Joe Apple had told me I didn't have much of that. And other store officials had bulwarked his opinion. Still, I had seen homely men walking the streets of El Paso's Little Chihuahua quarter with beautiful Mexican women, and no one could explain that either. Anyway, it was time for another walk. So I took one.

This time I trudged through Little Chihuahua, where both Miss Rosas and I lived. Little Chihuahua looked different to me that day. It was a broken-down Mexican quarter honeycombed with tenements, Mom and Pop groceries, herb shops, cafés, and spindly salt-cedar trees; with howling children running its streets and old Mexican revolutionaries sunning themselves on its curbs like iguanas.[6] But on that clear frosty day it was the world's most romantic place because Cecilia Rosas lived there.

While walking, I reasoned that Miss Rosas might want to go dancing after the movies. So I went to Professor Toribio Ortega's

[6] IGUANAS (ĭ·gwä′nəz): tropical American lizards.

dance studio and made arrangements to take my first lesson. Some neighborhood boys saw me when I came out. They bawled, *"Mariquita"* and made flutteringly effeminate motions, all vulgar if not obscene. It didn't matter. On my lunch hour I went back and took my first lesson anyway. Professor Ortega danced with me. Softened by weeks of dreaming, I went limp in his arms imagining he was Miss Rosas.

The rest of the day was the same as many others before it. As usual I spent most of it stealing glances at Miss Rosas and slipping up to the window ledge. She looked busy, efficient, not like a woman in love. Her many other admirers trooped to the water fountain to look at the way her black silk dress fitted her curves. Their profane admiration made me scowl even more than I usually did at such times.

When the day's work was done, I plodded home from the store just as dreamily as I had gone to it. Since I had no one else to confide in, I invited my oldest sister, Dulce Nombre de María, to go to the movies with me. They were showing Jorge Negrete and María Felix in *El Rapto* at the Colon Theater. It was a romantic movie, just the kind I wanted to see.

After it was over, I bought Dulce Nombre *churros* and hot *champurrado* at the Golden Taco Café. And I told my sister all about what had happened to me. She looked at me thoughtfully, then combed my hair back with her fingertips as though trying to soothe me. "Manito," she said, softly. "I wouldn't. . . ." Then she looked away and shrugged her shoulders.

On Monday I borrowed three dollars from my Uncle Rodolfo without telling him what it was for. Miss Rosas hadn't told me what night she wanted me to take her to the movies. But the way she had looked at me made me think that almost any night would do. So I decided on Friday. Waiting for it to come was hard. But I had to keep my mind occupied. So I went to Zamora's newsstand to get the Alma Norteña songbook. Poring through it for the most romantic song I could find, I decided on "La Cecilia."

All week long I practiced singing it on my way to school and in the shower after basketball practice with the Little Chihuahua Tigers at the Sagrado Corazón gym. But except for singing this song, I tried not to speak Spanish at all. At home I made my mother mad by saying in English, "Please pass the sugar."

My mother looked at me as though she couldn't believe what she had heard. Since my Uncle Rodolfo couldn't say anything more than "hello" and "good-bye" in English, he couldn't tell what I had said. So my sister Consuelo did.

"May the Dark Virgin with the benign look make this boy well enough to speak Christian again," my mother whispered.

This I refused to do. I went on speaking English even though my mother and uncle didn't understand it. This shocked my sisters as well. When they asked me to explain my behavior, I parroted Miss Rosas, saying, "We're living in the United States now."

My rebellion against being a Mexican created an uproar. Such conduct was unorthodox, if not scandalous, in a neighborhood where names like Burciaga, Rodríguez, and Castillo predominated. But it wasn't only the Spanish language that I lashed out against.

"Mother, why do we always have to eat *sopa, frijoles refritos, mondongo,* and *pozole?*" I complained. "Can't we ever eat roast beef or ham and eggs like Americans do?"

My mother didn't speak to me for two days after that. My Uncle Rodolfo grimaced and mumbled something about renegade Mexicans who want to eat ham and eggs even though the Montes Packing Company turned out the best *chorizo* this side of Toluca. My sister Consuelo giggled and called me a Rio Grande Irishman, an American Mister, a gringo, and a *bolillo.* Dulce Nombre looked at me worriedly.

Life at home was almost intolerable. Cruel jokes and mocking laughter made it so. I moped around looking sad as a day without bread. My sister Consuelo suggested I go to the courthouse and change my name to Beloved Wall, which is English for Amado Muro. My mother didn't agree. "If *Nuestro Señor*[7] had meant for Amadito to be an American, he would have given him a name like Smeeth or Jonesy," she said. My family was unsympathetic. With a family like mine, how could I ever hope to become an American and win Miss Rosas?

Friday came at last. I put on my only suit, slicked my hair down with liquid vaseline, and doused myself with Dulce Nombre's perfume.

[7] *Nuestro Señor:* Our Lord (Christ).

"Amado's going to serenade that pretty girl everyone calls La Americana," my sister Consuelo told my mother and uncle when I sat down to eat. "Then he's going to take her to the movies."

This made my uncle laugh and my mother scowl.

"*Qué pantalones tiene* (what nerve that boy's got)," my uncle said, "to serenade a twenty-year-old woman."

"La Americana," my mother said derisively. "That one's Mexican as pulque cured with celery."

They made me so nervous I forgot to take off my cap when I sat down to eat.

"Amado, take off your cap," my mother said. "You're not in La Lagunilla Market."

My uncle frowned. "All this boy thinks about is kissing girls," he said gruffly.

"But my boy's never kissed one," my mother said proudly.

My sister Consuelo laughed. "That's because they won't let him," she said.

This wasn't true. But I couldn't say so in front of my mother. I had already kissed Emalina Uribe from Porfirio Díaz Street not once but twice. Both times I'd kissed her in a darkened doorway less than a block from her home. But the kisses were over so soon we hardly had time to enjoy them. This was because Ema was afraid her big brother, the husky one nicknamed Toro, would see us. But if we'd had more time, it would have been better, I knew.

Along about six o'clock the three musicians who called themselves the Mariachis of Tecalitlán came by and whistled for me, just as they had said they would do. They never looked better than they did on that night. They had on black and silver charro uniforms and big black Zapata sombreros.[8]

My mother shook her head when she saw them. "Son, who ever heard of serenading a girl at six o'clock in the evening," she said. "When your father had the mariachis sing for me, it was always at two o'clock in the morning—the only proper time for a six-song *gallo.*"

But I got out my Ramírez guitar anyway. I put on my cap and rushed out to give the mariachis the money without even kissing

[8] ZAPATA SOMBREROS: hats named after the Mexican revolutionary leader Emilio Zapata (1877–1919).

my mother's hand or waiting for her to bless me. Then we headed for Miss Rosas' home. Some boys and girls I knew were out in the street. This made me uncomfortable. They looked at me wonderingly as I led the mariachi band to Miss Rosas' home.

A block away from Miss Rosas' home I could see her father, a grizzled veteran who fought for Pancho Villa,[9] sitting on the curb reading the Juárez newspaper, *El Fronterizo.*

The sight of him made me slow down for a moment. But I got back in stride when I saw Miss Rosas herself.

She smiled and waved at me. "Hello, Amadito," she said.

"Hello, Señorita Cecilia," I said.

She looked at the mariachis, then back at me.

"*Ay,* Amado, you're going to serenade your girl," she said. I didn't reply right away. Then when I was getting ready to say, "Señorita Cecilia, I came to serenade you," I saw the American man sitting in the sports roadster at the curb.

Miss Rosas turned to him. "I'll be right there, Johnny," she said.

She patted my cheek. "I've got to run now, Amado," she said. "Have a real nice time, darling."

I looked at her silken legs as she got into the car. Everything had happened so fast I was dazed. Broken dreams made my head spin. The contrast between myself and the poised American in the sports roadster was so cruel it made me wince.

She was happy with him. That was obvious. She was smiling and laughing, looking forward to a good time. Why had she asked me to take her to the movies if she already had a boyfriend? Then I remembered how the other salesladies had laughed, how I had wondered why they were laughing when they couldn't even hear what we were saying. And I realized it had all been a joke; everyone had known it but me. Neither Miss Rosas nor the other salesladies had ever dreamed I would think she was serious about wanting me to take her to the movies.

The American and Miss Rosas drove off. Gloomy thoughts oppressed me. They made me want to cry. To get rid of them I thought of going to one of the "bad death" cantinas in Juárez

[9] PANCHO VILLA: bandit chief and revolutionary leader who sought to control Mexico after the fall of President Díaz in 1910. He was ambushed and shot in 1923.

where tequila starts fights and knives finish them. There I could forget her in Jalisco-state style[10] with mariachis and tequila. Then I remembered I was so young that *cantineros* wouldn't serve me tequila.

So I thought some more. Emalina Uribe was the only other alternative. If we went over to Porfirio Díaz Street and serenaded her, I could go back to being a Mexican again. She was just as Mexican as I was, Mexican as *chicharrones.* I thought about smiling, freckle-faced Ema.

Ema wasn't like the Americana at all. She wore wash dresses that fitted loosely and even ate the *melcocha* candies Mexicans like so well on the street. On Sundays she wore a Zamora shawl to church, and her mother wouldn't let her use lipstick or let her put on high heels.

But with a brother like Toro, who didn't like me anyway, such a serenade might be more dangerous than romantic. Besides that, my faith in my looks, my character, or whatever it was that made women fall in love with men, was so undermined I could already picture her getting into a car with a handsome American just like Miss Rosas had done.

The Mariachis of Tecalitlán were getting impatient. They had been paid to sing six songs and they wanted to sing them. But they were all sympathetic. None of them laughed at me.

"Amado, don't look sad as I did the day I learned I'd never be a millionaire," the mariachi captain said, putting his arm around me. "If not that girl, then another."

But without Miss Rosas there was no one we could sing "La Cecilia" to. The street seemed bleak and empty now that she was gone. And I didn't want to serenade Ema Uribe, even though she hadn't been faithless as Miss Rosas had been. It was true she hadn't been faithless, but only lack of opportunity would keep her from getting into a car with an American, I reasoned cynically.

Just about then Miss Rosas' father looked up from his newspaper. He asked the mariachis if they knew how to sing "Cananea Jail." They told him they did. Then they looked at me. I thought it over for a moment. Then I nodded and started strumming the bass

[10] JALISCO-STATE STYLE: luxury associated with this state, in west central Mexico, whose capital is Guadalajara.

strings of my guitar. What had happened made it only too plain I could never trust Miss Rosas again. So we serenaded her father instead.

FOR DISCUSSION

1. Cecilia advises Amado to "speak English. And pronounce the words slowly and carefully, so you won't sound like a country Mexican." What do Amado's parents think of her advice? What do you think of it?

2. How would you describe Cecilia's character? Is she an admirable person? What is her attitude toward life? Do you agree with her attitude and with her behavior?

Arnulfo D. Trejo

b. 1922

Arnulfo Trejo was brought up in Arizona and educated at the University of Arizona in Tucson. After college, he moved to California, where he worked as a librarian at Long Beach City College. Like most Mexican-American fiction writers after World War II, Trejo has written about life in the city and the interesting personalities who live there. Arturo Ramírez, the maistro *in Trejo's story, is a fascinating character who never lets the problems of the world get him down. In his barber shop his customers get more than a haircut; they get a philosophy of life.*

Maistro

Early one evening when I had missed getting through the closing door of my regular barber shop in downtown Santa Monica, I paid my first visit to Arturo Ramírez. His shop is located on Olympic Boulevard, where a group of small businesses had been established to serve what few people of Mexican descent live in the community. The shop is flanked by a tavern on one side and a small grocery store with an adjoining pool hall on the other.

From the very first time I drove down Olympic, that section of West Los Angeles had aroused my curiosity, possibly because of my own Mexican heritage. Yet I never took the time to stop, for I was usually rushing to and from work.

This time, however, I needed a haircut badly, and I was determined to get it. When I first went in, a short, dark-complexioned, gray-haired man wearing a white jacket greeted me with a jovial *"Buenas tardes, señor. Pase, pase."* I in turn gave him a hesitant smile and a nod of the head and continued to walk to a nearby table. I picked up a beat-up magazine and sat down in a vacant chair facing the barber.

Presently, I looked up from my reading to see how many more customers were ahead of me. The barber, who was now looking at me in the large mirror in front of him, interrupted his conversation to say, "There're three ahead of you. Those two there just come here to play cards and wear out the chairs." Then he burst into laughter.

As I did not find his remark especially funny, I moved to whisper to the person next to me: "Hope the old boy hasn't been hitting the bottle, 'cause I'd hate to have him work on me with that mean-looking blade he's got."

"Mister," my listener broke in, showing some resentment at what I had said, "I never seen that man act no other way. Furthermore, he don't need the stuff to be happy. Still, Maistro always has joy in his heart and a kind word for everyone."

After those words of enlightenment about the barber, I slid down in my chair to hide my red face behind a magazine.

As I waited for my turn, I observed that everyone addressed the barber as *maistro,* just as the Negro had done. *Maistro* is a dialect form of the Spanish *maestro* meaning teacher, master workman, or skilled artisan.

This form of addressing someone was not new to me, since it is quite common in Mexico, where the master workman in any vocation is usually referred to as *maistro,* especially if he is well along in years. It was strange, though, to note the respect which this word carried here. There was even more than respect. Endearment, perhaps, may best describe the sentiment attached to *maistro.*

More and more I became interested in the little man behind the barber's chair. He appeared to know many of his customers by name, the kinds of work they did, and, as they confided in him, their personal problems. I overheard a young man tell him the difficulties that he was having in getting married. By the time the haircut was over, the boy looked happier and much relieved.

"Sure you won't forget, Maistro?" the boy asked as he started to leave.

The barber said nothing, but looked at him with a reassuring smile.

Weeks later I discovered that Ramírez became the boy's *padrino* or sponsor, which meant, among other things, asking for the hand of the bride-to-be and contributing to the financing of the wedding.

When my turn came to get a haircut, I was bulging with curiosity. But I sat patiently, hoping that Maistro would start the conversation. He did—by explaining that most barbers talked too much.

"Sometimes it is forgotten that the customers are tired and would prefer to get their haircuts without someone blasting their eardrums," he remarked.

When he noticed that I was not going to say anything, he continued by saying that he was no exception.

I interrupted to explain that if I was keeping quiet, it was merely to give him a chance to talk, and stressed that I would very much like to have him tell me about himself. But despite my obvious sincerity, it was difficult to get him to say much. Then, too, there was interference from outside.

Someone going by would tap on the window and holler, "Hello, Maistro!" "*Hola,* Maistro!" Or simply "Hi, Maistro!" Others would take the time to step in for a few words.

In between greetings I learned from the little man in the white jacket that he had been doing business in that same place for the last twenty-nine years. His home had been in Mexico City, where he started as a barber, and where his experience with the *turistas norteamericanos* had not been too pleasant. That is, until he met a certain Mr. Johnson, who not only convinced him that Americans were not such a bad lot, but also sold him on the idea of coming to the States.

While putting the finishing touches to my haircut he uttered almost to himself, "Yes, after all these years in this country, I, too, can say that Americans are not such a bad lot. Right, Billy?"

The man called Billy had been dozing away on one of the chairs. He showed every sign of being an alcoholic.

Before I left, the barber extended his hand for me to shake. It was a parting of two friends.

On my way home I had a feeling of satisfaction, of contentment . . . something about that man stayed with me.

The next time I needed a haircut, I intended to go to my regular barber. I even drove twice around the block on which his shop was located. But when I could not find a parking space, I drove three miles to Arturo's shop.

It was my morning off, and I had anticipated that I would not have long to wait. At that time of day barber shops are seldom busy. To my astonishment this one did not even have a barber, but it was open.

Just as I was about to leave, I noticed two men heading in the direction of the barber shop. When they came in, both gladly volunteered to tell me what had happened.

It turned out that Billy had been found lying in the back alley and had almost been carried off by a patrol car. To convince the police that Billy was simply enjoying a little morning nap, Ramírez had offered to take him to his own home.

When the barber came back, he greeted us as if nothing had happened, took his regular place, and called out, "Next?"

On this occasion our conversation was mostly about Billy. I guess I started it when I asked him why Billy did not go to a sanitarium or a hospital.

"Oh, Billy has been to hospitals all right," Ramírez answered. "And seventeen years ago when I first met him, I even tried to cure him myself. Now all I do is keep him out of trouble when I can and help him buy a drink when he's got the shakes bad."

I should have liked to stay longer to talk to my friend, but I was late already. The moment I went out the door, though, I began looking forward to my next haircut.

Two weeks later I was back again. It was a Saturday morning, and Ramírez was still tidying up the place. Once we had exchanged our customary greetings, I took my place in the chair, and the barber proceeded to do his job.

Soon afterwards, two fellows looking like a pair of truck drivers who had been on the road all night stepped in to await their turn. They seemed tired and sleepy but appeared to be in a cheerful mood. One of them even joked about the barber's lack of good taste in art. "Pictures and more pictures of bullfighters and not even one of Marilyn Monroe," he said laughingly.

About that time a Negro boy poked his head through the door and inquired, "Maistro, how many more?"

"Two more, George, two more," answered the barber.

"Right, man. Be right back," replied the kid as he went away.

Suddenly the two customers who had been waiting jumped to their feet. "You're not going to give that black so-and-so a haircut, are you, mister?" one of them asked.

Ramírez looked startled for a second. Then, without even looking at his interrogators, he disappeared through the back door.

When he dashed back, he was clutching something in his left hand. It was hair that looked as if it had come out of a garbage can.

No one said a word. The barber looked excited, but his hands were steady as he carefully sorted the hair by its color and laid it on the table in little bunches. After that was completed, he stretched his arms as if about to perform an important surgical operation, clicked his scissors in the air a few times, and then began to clip a little off each bunch of hair.

When Ramírez finished cutting the last hairs which he held between his fingers, he broke the silence by saying, "You see, these scissors don't know the difference between blond, brown, or black hair. Why, this is such a good brand of scissors that they can even cut curly or straight hair."

At that point he let out his usual hearty laugh and continued with my haircut.

"Still think you don't know much about art, Barber," one of the fellows exclaimed, "but I grant you've got a point this time." Then turning to his friend, he asked, "You still want a haircut?"

"You heard what the man said, didn't ya?" the other replied. "He's got a good pair of shears there." The two of them started laughing, and pretty soon all four of us were laughing together.

"Next . . . ?"

FOR DISCUSSION

1. Compare Ramírez with another barber, Señor Garza, in the Mario Suarez story on page 99.

2. Are Ramírez and his way of life in danger of becoming obsolete, like Gonzalo and Killer in the story "Maestria"? If this were true, what would be the consequences?

Alfredo Otero y Herrera

b. 1932

Alfredo Otero y Herrera was born in Jerome, Arizona. He traveled widely as a young man, attending universities in the United States, Spain, and Mexico, and is presently Associate Professor of Hispanic Literature at California State College, Los Angeles. In the following story, Herrera describes a boy's childhood experience which is bound to affect his view of life as an adult.

The Bending of a Twig

Ralph shooed the flies away from the screen door before he hurried into the back porch. He set the groceries down on the rickety table covered with a worn, red-checked oilcloth. As he did, the bag split, sending apples bouncing off the table onto a heap of dirty clothes that lay on the floor.

"I'm home, mother," he cried.

Ralph's mother, wearing a faded cotton print dress, came out of the kitchen. She was a tall, gaunt woman in her early forties with dark circles under her eyes and an enormous pile of disheveled gray hair. Her husband, a happy-go-lucky bartender, had died of pneumonia the previous winter. Unable to find work in Roswell because of his reputation for drinking more than he served, he had gone to Portales to tend bar in the Elks Club. He had written to her several times, telling her that he would send for her and the boys as soon as he had the money. But he had died suddenly, leaving her penniless. Not knowing how to do anything else, she began washing the clothes for the bachelors of Roswell and those families who could afford to have their laundry done for them. She worked from dawn far into the night every day, washing, ironing, and mending in order to support herself and her two sons, Leo, twelve, and Ralph, ten. She complained constantly of headaches, telling her sons that she would probably die soon too.

As she reached under her dress to adjust the strap of her undergarments that were always slipping from her shoulders, she inspected the contents of the grocery bag.

"My god, Ralphie, did you have to go and bust the bag?"

"It wasn't my fault. The apples was wet and made it bust," he pleaded.

"Did you get the starch?" she asked, taking the groceries from the ripped bag.

"Jeez, mom. I plum forgot."

"My god, can't you do nothing right? Where's the change?"

"What change?" he replied, with his eyes directed to the floor.

"What change?" she screamed as she pulled the yellow-gray hair from about her face. "I gave you a five-dollar bill, and I know that it came to only $4.80. Where's the receipt?"

She crossed to him, forced his head back, and grabbed him by the shoulders. Ralph's face puckered, straining, trying not to cry.

"Did you stop by the Chocolate Shop and spend it?"

Ralph tried to lower his head again, but she snapped it back up.

"I met Lalo García," he said, trying to control the quivering of his chin.

"That dirty Mexican. I told you to stay away from that cheap trash, didn't I?"

She jerked his ear severely, causing him to burst into tears.

"By god, you're going to get a beating for this."

"But mother, the groceries cost $4.95, and I thought you wouldn't care."

"Wouldn't care about what?" she hissed, giving his ear another sharp pull.

"Wouldn't care if I spent the nickel for a Coke. I was thirsty," he sobbed.

"Why didn't you get a drink from the fountain in front of the courthouse if you was thirsty?"

"It's broke," he choked. "Ol' man Gardner is fixing it and said we couldn't have no water."

"You're lying to me, Ralph, just like your dad did, 'cause I seen Gardner drive past the house on his way to the slaughterhouse about an hour ago."

"Honest, mother, I did talk with him."

"You're going to get a beating for this. First you steal from your own mother, run around with dirty Mexican trash, and now you go and lie to me."

Ralph's face turned white; then he ran into the tiny bedroom adjoining the back porch screaming, "I'm not lying. Honest, mother, I'm not lying."

His mother pulled a worn slipper from her right foot and went after him.

Ralph gave a sharp cry as he bumped his head on the iron railing in his effort to crawl under the bed and to temporary safety. He huddled in the corner under the bed, pressing close to the wall. His head hurt him. He pressed his face to the green-and-yellow flowered linoleum. The lint and dust that had gathered there made him sneeze. It frightened him. He felt helpless waiting.

His mother strode into the room and stood at the foot of the bed, shouting, "Come out from under that bed, Ralph, or you're going to get a worse beating."

"No," he muttered weakly.

"Ralph! Do as I say!" she screamed again.

He could see the lower parts of her bare legs streaked with the angry blue varicose veins. He thought them ugly and wondered why they were there, what he had done, why she was going to beat him. The prospect of the beating caused him to burst into tears anew. He saw her feet shift and heard her call out to his elder brother who had just entered the back porch.

"Leo, go get me the razor strop. I'm really going to teach him a lesson."

At the mentioning of the razor strop he stopped crying in fear and called timidly, "I'm sorry, mother. I won't do it again."

In reply he heard his brother's footsteps retreating to the far side of the porch where the strop hung on the wall next to the fly swatter. He seemed to return so quickly.

"Help me move the bed," she commanded his brother.

The bed was rolled back, squeaking on its rusty casters.

Ralph, realizing he couldn't escape, rose slowly and stood before her submissively, trying to smile in hopes that she wouldn't beat him. She grabbed his arm and dragged him onto the porch. He looked at his brother, as if for help, but Leo only winced and swallowed hard.

"Now, are you ever going to lie to me again? Or steal?" she hissed as she brought the strop down hard against the back of his legs. "Are you? Huh? Are you?"

Ralph let out a piercing scream. He threw his right hand in front of his face in protection as he hopped wildly in his efforts to escape the blows that fell on his skinny body. He seemed to be dancing around his mother as if she were a Maypole. His head was thrown back; his mouth was opened as widely as it could. The lips, drawn tightly over his teeth, had turned a pale blue. He wasn't screaming any more. So great was his crying that he only made guttural sounds as he tried to get his breath. He threw himself upon the floor, falling on the cat's saucer full of milk, kicking his feet frantically, as she hit him for the last time.

Leo, witnessing the beating, let out an embarrassed giggle. She turned on him and spat, "Do you want some too? Get in there and do those dishes!"

"But I didn't do nothing, mother," he whined.

She motioned as if to strike him.

"Get in there and do those dishes!"

He ran into the kitchen, slamming the door after him.

She walked over to where Ralph lay.

"Get up!" she ordered him.

He got up crying loudly, his back hunched over—cowering from her.

"Are you going to lie to me again?" she asked, advancing towards him. She paused momentarily to get her breath.

"And if I ever hear of you with that dirty Mexican again, you're going to get another beating. Do you hear?"

Sobbing uncontrollably, he scrambled over the pile of dirty clothes and rushed out of the porch into the hot afternoon sun to the woodshed with its rotting boards and rusty tin roof. The bright sun blinded him, adding to his misery. The rain of the night before had made the air so humid and heavy that when he entered the shed, he caught his breath. But he welcomed its darkness. Susie, his cat, lay asleep on a mound of dirt made damp by the rain that had seeped through the numerous holes in the roof. Leaving the door partly open, he went to the coal bin and sat on its edge. He hoisted his pant leg. The red welts glared at him. He rubbed saliva over the welts, hoping to soothe them. They were painful. He let his pant leg drop, and holding out his hand, called to his cat.

"Here, Susie. Here, Susie. Nice kitty-kitty. Nice kitty."

The cat stretched luxuriously and came to him slowly. Gently the cat sniffed his fingertips. He reached out to pick her up, but she drew back quickly.

"Here, Susie. Nice, nice Susie," he pleaded.

Once again she sniffed his fingertips. This time he snatched her up before she could get away and pressed her tightly to his chest.

"You love me, don't you, Susie? I won't hurt you, will I?" he asked, stroking the back of her head.

Whipping her tail furiously and yowling unhappily, she dug her claws into his shoulder. Letting out a surprised cry, he leaped up and flung the cat away from him. She darted toward the door, stopping at the threshold, her tail still whipping back and forth.

"You don't love me either, you dirty cat!" he said as he picked up a small piece of coal and threw it at her. The coal smashed against the door, frightening Susie out of the shed and out of sight.

"Nobody loves me. Nobody."

With a weary sigh he sat on the dirt floor and leaned against the bin. He wiped his nose on his shirt sleeve, and resting his head against the dirty black boards, closed his eyes. Soon he was sound asleep.

"What you doing in here?" his brother asked, awakening him.

"Nothing."

"I've been looking all over for you for the past half hour," he said, staring at his brother. "Jeez, Ralphie, you're going to sweat yourself to death. Besides, mother has been calling you."

"What does she want?"

"You're supposed to go to confession this afternoon. Jeez, Ralphie, you've done spoiled your shirt. You put it on clean only this morning."

"It was dirty anyhow. I got Susie's milk all over it. Is mother still mad?"

"I don't know. She went over to see Mrs. Collins so as she could use her phone." He dug his feet into the soft dirt, then added, "You had better get inside the house and take a bath before she comes back."

"O.K."

He stood up and brushed the dirt off the back of his trousers. The perspiration ran down the sides of his face into the hollow of his neck, leaving streaks where it had washed away the dirt and coal dust.

"If you hurry, I'll let you wear my tee shirt."

"I don't want to wear it."

"Why not? You were mad 'cause I wouldn't let you wear it yesterday."

"So what?"

"Come on, Ralphie! I'll race you to the house," he yelled, pulling him out of the woodshed.

Ralph jerked away from him violently.

"Quit pushing me, damn you, and leave me alone!"

Frightened by his own outburst, he ran into the house and locked himself in the bathroom. He washed his face and hands, dried them on a washrag, then left the house and walked to the church. When he reached it, he sat on the stone wall and looked up at the white statue of the Virgin Mary set above the doorway. He had always liked the smile on her face. He wondered what she was doing now. He climbed down from the fence and entered the church. He genuflected, crossed himself with holy water, and half-kneeled and half-sat in a back pew. He recited the Act of Contrition mechanically, then tried to number the sins he had committed as the sisters had told him to do. But the memory of the beating brought him close to tears. His chin started to quiver. He looked around quickly, embarrassed as if someone might have seen him; but no one had. He left the pew for the confessional. There was only one other in line—Mrs. Soltero. She was dressed in black, as were most of the old Mexican women in town. Her black shawl that covered her head almost reached the wooden floor. Her back was bent with age, making her no taller than Ralph. He watched her wipe the perspiration from her face and finger the bright blue beads of her rosary rapidly. She paid no attention to him. He remembered seeing her boiling clothes in a blackened tub in her back yard when he and Leo had gone to look for Coke bottles in the town dump. She entered the booth after Mrs. McDevitt, the fat lady who always sang the loudest during Benediction. His heart began to beat rapidly at the thought of being next. He stared hard at the floor and prayed that Mrs. Soltero would stay in a long time. He looked up and saw her come out.

His heart pounded as he entered the hot, dark confessional booth. He kneeled on the hard wood floor, crossing himself hurriedly as he did so. The booth, smelling strongly of garlic and human sweat, nearly suffocated him. He looked at the cheap plastic crucifix nailed on the wall and at the priest's profile outlined on the white cloth that was draped before the screen. He closed his eyes tightly.

"Forgive me, Father, for I have sinned."

"When was your last confession?"

"Two weeks ago."

He faltered, not knowing what to say next.

"Well, son, come on. Do you want me to confess for you?"

Now his temples throbbed with the beating of his heart.

"No, Father."

He squeezed his hands together tightly and leaned against the wall.

"I hate my mother," he said breathlessly.

"What did you say?" whispered the priest.

"I hate my mother," he repeated weakly.

"You don't mean that, son. You're just upset. What did she do? Spank you?"

"Yes." The tears started to come. He fought them. "She spanks me all the time."

"Well, you must do something to make her spank you. Now don't you?"

"She said that I lied and stole from her, but I didn't and she knew it."

He began to cry softly.

"Come now, you must have done something. She wouldn't spank

you for no reason at all."

"She did. She wouldn't believe me. She said that I stole her grocery change today."

"Did you?"

"No, I only spent it on a Coke," he said between sobs.

"Why did you do that? Did you have her permission?"

Ralph tried to answer but couldn't.

The priest asked again, "Did you have her permission?"

"No. I was thirsty. I didn't steal from her."

"It was her money, wasn't it? You didn't have permission to spend her money, did you?"

"No."

"How old are you, son?"

"Ten."

"You're old enough to know that you have to have permission. Now you don't want to be a bad boy and do things like that, do you? Jesus doesn't like for us to do things like that."

"I'm not a bad boy!"

"Calm down, son. Don't raise your voice. Remember there are others outside."

"No. I hate her. She doesn't love me," he said, crying uncontrollably, "and you don't believe me either."

"Shh. Please."

"I hate her! I hate you!" he sobbed, his voice rising steadily in pitch. "Nobody believes me!"

He scrambled to his feet and pushed wildly at the door, causing it to bang loudly against the back pew. He rushed hysterically out of the church toward the railroad tracks that would eventually lead to his house.

Upon reaching home he stood near the clump of hollyhocks which grew by the side of the house. His mother had recently poured water on them. The water had hit an anthill nearby. He watched the ants swarm frantically over the hole. He wondered why they were so silent. He heard his mother singing "Ramona" to herself as she scrubbed clothes on the washboard. He stood listening intently until she had ceased the scrubbing, wrung out the clothes, and gone into the back yard to hang them to dry. He slipped unnoticed into the house and into the bathroom. He washed his face and combed his thick black hair carefully. He heard his mother enter the back porch and shout at his brother to not let the beans burn. When he entered the back porch, his mother was sorting a new bundle of laundry. She looked at him as she searched the pockets of a pair of khaki trousers and asked, "Well, did you go to confession?"

Ralph leaned over a rinsing tub and plunged his hands into the water. Avoiding his mother's gaze, he contemplated his hands through the water tinted with bluing and answered, "Yes, mother; he made me say ten Our Fathers and ten Hail Marys for my penance."

FOR DISCUSSION

1. Do you think Ralph and his family are Mexican-Americans? If so, how do you explain the mother's warning to Ralph to stay away from Mexicans?

2. Is Ralph really treated unfairly? Who is to blame for his problems?

3. How does the story's title relate to its theme?

Nick C. Vaca

b. 1943

Nick Vaca, born in Deming, New Mexico, attended the University of California and the University of Nottingham, England. He is now back in California, where he is on the staff of the Mexican-American journal El Grito. *"The Purchase" is a bitter account of the mistreatment an elderly Mexican-American woman receives from mistrusting Anglos. The story leaves little doubt as to why some Mexican-Americans are reluctant to leave the* barrio.

The Purchase

"*Ave Maria Purísma,* I must make another *pago hoy*[1] or else it'll be too late. Sí, too late, and then what would I do? Christmas is so close, and if I don't hurry *con los pagos,* I'll have nothing to give any of *mis hijos.*[2] If that should happen, it would weigh *muy pesado*[3] on my mind. Even now, *con el pensamiento* that I may not be able to give them anything, I have trouble *durmiendo en la noche.*[4] And, Santo Niño de Atocha, if Christmas should come

[1] *Ave Maria Purísima, pago hoy:* Hail, Mary most pure . . . payment today.

[2] *con los pagos, mis hijos:* with the payments . . . my children.

[3] *muy pesado:* very heavy.

[4] *con el pensamiento, durmiendo en la noche:* with the thought . . . sleeping in the night.

and catch me *sin nada,* I would never sleep well *por el resto de mi vida.*"[5]

Sitting on a large, bulky sofa, its brown cover worn and frayed at the arm rests and back, Doña Lupe was thinking over the progress she had made in her Christmas shopping. Surrounded by the wrinkles of her small, sad face, two dark eyes closed and opened intermittently as her gray head nodded in deep absorption, figuring the amount of time and money she needed to complete her shopping. Becoming agitated with pleasure and anxiety, she lifted her thin body off the sofa, wrapped her faded green sweater around her waist, and began shuffling from one end of the three-room apartment to the other as she tightly pursed her thin lips and placed her gathered fingers on her sunken cheeks, again losing herself in a world of calculations. As she reached the far end of her apartment, she stopped at the bay window, gathered her arms about herself, and dropped her head slightly to one side. Outside the sky was a cold gray with the dark clouds and fog combining to form low, dark shadows that covered Stockton as far as Doña Lupe could see. Below her apartment an elm tree with morning dewdrops still fresh on its naked branches began to sway slightly as the first gush of cold morning wind disturbed its somnolent serenity, causing Doña Lupe to shiver slightly. Shuffling to the kitchen table, she sat down and pulled a grease-spotted piece of brown paper out of her apron pocket. Clearing the salt shaker, a bowl of *chile salsa,* and some cold tortillas that remained from last evening's dinner, Doña Lupe placed the paper on the table. As she squinted under the light of the naked light bulb that hung directly overhead, her fingers underlined names and *x*'s on the paper. The names were those of her children, and the *x*'s indicated who had been bought a gift. The names were meaningless. That is, they meant a great deal to her, but she did not know them. Doña Lupe could not read. But she had memorized them in the order that they appeared on the paper after having Antonio, her youngest son, read them over and over to her during the past two months; so now, even if she didn't know how to read, she knew for whom the various scrawlings stood. The list began with Gilbert, her eldest son, and ended with Gloria, her youngest daughter, and

[5] *sin nada, por el resto de mi vida:* without anything . . . for the rest of my life.

everyone but Rudy who was in the army had the large, dark, trembling *x* of her black grease pencil.

Had anyone told Doña Lupe five years ago when her husband died that she would be able to buy store gifts for her children, she would have shaken her head in polite disagreement. Her monthly welfare allowance only covered the necessities that life imposed on her—the rent of her apartment, her food, clothing, and her weekly movie at the Mexican movie house every Saturday with Doña Pifora, another widow who met her necessities in the same manner. To even think that she would ever be able to buy store gifts for her children was very much out of the question. As Doña Lupe reasoned, either she had to come into a lot of money, or she would have to buy on credit. The chances of her coming into a lot of money did not even occupy her thoughts, and credit, well, that was something that only people with money could afford. So she contented herself with giving her daughters colorfully embroidered dish towels, and inexpensive handkerchiefs to her sons. That's the way it had been for the past five years, ever since her husband's death, when a lack of money and friends had driven her to her apartment and her daily existence. And so it would have probably continued until her death, had she not sighed during one of her Saturday movie dates with Doña Pifora.

"*Ay*, Doña Pifora, Christmas is coming again, and I have to start making *mis hijos* something again. I'm getting tired of giving them the same thing year after year. I know they don't mind my presents, but I do. You know how it is; you have *hijos* of your own; it's not like you're ignorant of the matter."

Doña Pifora nodded in agreement.

"It's difficult to explain," continued Doña Lupe, "but when you don't give your *hijos* anything for Christmas, you don't feel good inside. My *hijos* tell me that it doesn't matter, that I shouldn't even think about giving gifts to so many of them. They say it's silly what I do every year, but I still feel bad if I can't give them anything for Christmas. Christmas is special, and special times shouldn't go unnoticed."

"Well," inquired Doña Pifora, "why don't you give them gifts from the store? They're right, you know. It's too much what you do for them each year," added Doña Pifora cautiously.

"Why?" answered Doña Lupe. "You know that all my money,

every bit of it, is used *en la casa.*[6] For food, *la renta,* some clothing, things like that. That's why. I don't have money to go around buying store presents."

"Of course you do," countered Doña Pifora; "everybody does. Listen, it's clear you haven't heard of lay-away," Doña Pifora declared so loudly that several people in the foyer of the theater turned and looked at them.

"Lay-away, *¿qué es eso?*"[7] inquired Doña Lupe.

"It's like credit," proceeded Doña Pifora, "but not really credit. That is, it works almost the same. What you do is this. You go to a store that has lay-away and look around. If you find something you like, you just take it to the counter and tell the lady you want to buy it, but that you don't have enough money and that you would like it put on lay-away. Then you give the lady about fifty cents or whatever you have. Then every week or when you have money, you give them what you can. The only thing is that you can't have the thing you want until you pay for it."

"What?" asked Doña Lupe.

"Oh, *sí;* until you finish the payments, you can't have it," answered Doña Pifora.

"Well, that's not too bad, I guess," said Doña Lupe. "After all, it's only fair that they should keep the things until you finish paying for them. It's the only right thing to do."

"Where do they have this lay-away, Doña Pifora?" inquired Doña Lupe.

"Well, I always do my lay-away at Clifford's; you know, the store on the big street with the large trees across from the big hotel," answered Doña Pifora.

"Clifford's, eh?" added Doña Lupe softly, almost to herself.

Though Doña Lupe feigned a mild interest in the lay-away plan, her heart was beating furiously with excitement at the prospect that for the first time in five years she would have a chance to give her children some store-bought presents. What she had told Doña Pifora about needing all her money was true. But for store gifts she would sacrifice a little. Perhaps she didn't have to eat as well, not buy any clothes for a while, and give up her Saturday

[6] *en la casa:* at home.

[7] *¿qué es eso:* what is that?

movies. That would be the most painful sacrifice, but she would do it.

It was on a cold and windy October morning when Doña Lupe set out for Clifford's, a dollar in her apron pocket and a head full of dreams. As she shuffled past children playing in the park near her house, the autumn leaves swirled about her feet, and the crisp morning air foretold the coming of winter. Clifford's was a variety store of the sort that sold most anything, and the anything it sold was generally of poor quality. It was to this store that most of the pensioners and mothers on welfare came to buy their clothing, ironing boards, sweets, and the other necessities that the corner grocery store could not provide. In short, it was the type of store that can be found in almost any small town in the San Joaquin Valley. Catering to the poor and aged, Clifford's reflected its attitude toward its clientele in the arrangement and treatment of its goods. Shoes were thrown in with plastic balls, Orlon sweaters were placed alongside cans of paint; potted plants were surrounded by greeting cards, and the floor was unswept. The clerks were generally fresh out of high school, and even if they had worked at Clifford's for years, they still looked as if they were fresh out of high school. They chewed gum as they arranged items on counters and engaged in conversation with each other while they waited on customers. The boys would shoulder each other as they worked in pairs along the aisles. The young girls would constantly pat their hair to ensure its perfection.

Ambling along the aisles looking cautiously at items, even daring to touch and examine them, Doña Lupe attempted to settle in her mind that the explanation Doña Pifora had made of the lay-away was both real and accurate, and what she saw could be hers. Whatever doubts she had about the existence of lay-away were dispelled by the sense of exhilaration that she could own what she saw. Her eyes moved rapidly, selecting items with her eyes tightened to cover the smile that strove to break through all her restraint. For Ruth she chose a black porcelain cat with diamond eyes that sparkled nicely when they were held against the light; for Felicia she chose a bouquet of plastic flowers; for Antonio she chose a gold-colored key chain; for Antonia she chose a porcelain collie dog, and so it went until all ten children had been selected presents. Cradling them in her arms, she carefully placed them one by one on the counter as the clerk, a girl of about eighteen years with pimples and heavy make-up, began to examine them. Before the girl could begin totaling the items, the words *lay-away* slipped from Doña Lupe's mouth. The young girl's forehead furrowed.

"What?" she said.

"Lay-away," blurted Doña Lupe.

"Oh yeah, wait a minute, huh," mumbled the girl.

Turning towards the back of the store, the girl shouted, "Oh, Mr. Clifford, this Mexican woman wants this stuff on lay-away."

From behind the candy counter a tall man, with thinning hair, wire-rim glasses, a large straight nose, and a pale, colorless face approached Doña Lupe.

"Want this stuff on lay-away, huh?" he asked.

"Lay-away," repeated Doña Lupe. Her English was limited, but she felt that lay-away was all the man needed to know. If such a thing existed, she knew that it would be self-explanatory. If it didn't exist, it was no use trying to explain how it worked, especially if she had to refer to Doña Pifora. Because if lay-away didn't exist, then how would he know about Doña Pifora?

"Yeah, all right," said the tall man in a resigned tone.

The items, all of them, totaled twenty-five dollars. Writing out a receipt for the items, the tall man placed them in a cardboard box, taped the receipt on the box, and placed it underneath the counter; then he turned to Doña Lupe and said, "How much you gonna put down?"

Doña Lupe reached into her apron pocket and pulled out the crumpled dollar she had saved in the last week and placed it on the counter.

"Just one dollar. That all you gonna put down?" inquired the man.

Doña Lupe nodded her head.

"Well, if that's all you got, that's all you got," said the tall man philosophically as he placed the dollar in the cash register.

"You know the deal," continued the tall man; "come in every week and give a dollar or whatever you got to give, and when you finish paying the twenty-five dollars, then you get the stuff. Okay?"

Doña Lupe nodded her head and shuffled out the door happy

that the October wind was cold, the sun bright, and that winter was on its way.

That had occurred two months ago, or as Doña Lupe counted, eight payments ago. Now all she had left to pay was $6.43, and today was the ninth week of her payments. This week she planned to pay three dollars, which she had saved by . . . well, modesty hoards that secret, and next week she planned to pay the remaining amount.

As she reached the kitchen table for the fifth time in her pacing, Doña Lupe stopped and noticed that the clock showed eight. She put on her heavy coat, placed a black scarf on her head, and stepped into the dull December day with the fog still hanging low and the houses and trees shivering in the damp morning. The thought that this was the second to the last payment gave her a feeling of modest satisfaction that even such a sad morning could not dispel. As was now the custom, when she made her payments, she was usually the only customer in the store at such an early hour. Following her usual routine, she located the tall man in the back of the store and paid her three dollars; but instead of leaving the store as was her usual fashion, she lingered along the aisles looking and holding things that caught her attention—plastic flowers, small, furry dogs that squealed when squeezed and made Doña Lupe smile, sweaters, velvet ribbons. Having satisfied her curiosity, she slowly shuffled out the door. As she began crossing the street, her right arm was grabbed and a nervous but firm voice said, "All right, lady, what you got?"

Doña Lupe turned to see a tall, redheaded boy wearing the familiar green smock that all Clifford's employees were made to wear. The boy could not have been over seventeen years, and his young face showed a combination of determination and confusion. Doña Lupe was dumfounded.

"Yeah, don't act dumb; what you got? What's under the coat? I know it's there. You weren't walking around for so long for nothing. I had my eye on you. Come on, now; what is it? We get your kind all the time. Walk around acting dumb and then pinch something like nothing happened."

Flustered from embarrassment and hurt at the thought that she should be accused of stealing, Doña Lupe simply stared at the young man. In her sixty-eight years of life she had never stolen a thing, and to be accused of such an act was the most horrible thing she could imagine. She held herself stiffly.

"All right; since you're not gonna talk, then let's see what you got."

The young man flung open her coat to find that she had stolen nothing. A sheepish grin came over his face; he muttered something and quickly went inside the store.

Doña Lupe could not bear the thought of being accused of stealing. She wept quietly all the way home. Arriving at her apartment, she took off her coat but left her scarf on and began to pace the floor again. It was one o'clock in the morning when she finally stopped pacing, sat down on the brown sofa, and began embroidering dish towels.

FOR DISCUSSION

1. Why did the clerk suspect Doña Lupe of stealing?

2. What was her reaction to the accusation? At the end of the story, why does Doña Lupe start embroidering dish towels?

3. What is suggested about the Mexican-American's experience in American society?

Richard Olivas

b. 1946

"My name is Richard Olivas and I am 25 years of age. I was born a Chicano on March 10, 1946. My parents are financially poor. They were migrant farm workers for about twelve years till they settled in San Jose in 1945. After that time my father worked as a construction laborer and my mother as a cannery worker. My father is 68 and my mother 64 years old, and they are currently living on welfare.

"I have twelve brothers and sisters; half of them have been in and out of prisons and jails ever since I can remember. How I managed to stay out of the joint I'll never know. I also wonder how I ever made it to college; not because I wasn't smart enough, rather I wonder how I got in in spite of the inadequate counseling and education I received in grade school. When I started college, it would take me about half an hour to read a textbook paragraph. I've improved since, but only because I found out how important learning can be, and reading is a means to a certain type of learning experience. I recently graduated from San Jose State. Did I learn anything? Yes, that 'higher education' is also inadequate.

"I am now working out of Economic and Social Opportunities, Inc., a poverty program in San Jose.

"In the fall semester '68 at San Jose College I wrote the poem 'The Immigrant Experience.' It is my experience. It is the Chicano experience."

The Immigrant Experience

I'm sitting in my history class,
The instructor commences rapping,
I'm in my U.S. History class,
And I'm on the verge of napping.

The Mayflower landed on Plymouth Rock.
Tell me more! Tell me more!
Thirteen colonies were settled.
I've heard it all before.

What did he say?
Dare I ask him to reiterate?
Oh, why bother,
It sounded like he said,
George Washington's my father.

I'm reluctant to believe it,
I suddenly raise my *mano.*
If George Washington's my father,
Why wasn't he Chicano?

FOR DISCUSSION

Why is the student in the poem bored by his U.S. History class? What is the poet's message?

Spanish Words and Phrases

amorcito, –ta (ah-mor-see'to, – tah) little love
¡ay! (eye) oh! (exclamation used to express strong emotion)
barrio (bar' ree-o) one of the districts into which a large town or city is divided; neighborhood
bolero (bo-lay'ro) stately Spanish dance
bolillo (bo-lee'yo) starched lace cuff; English-speaking person
buenas tardes (boo-ay'nahs tar'days) good afternoon
cañada (cah-nyah'dah) gully; ravine
cantina (cahn-tee'nah) barroom; tavern
caporal (cah-po-rahl') boss of a cowboy outfit
cautivo, –va (cah-oo-tee'vo, –vah) captive; prisoner
centavo (sen-tah'vo) coin worth one hundredth of a peso
champurrado (chahm-poor-rah'do) drink made of corn gruel and chocolate
charro (char'ro) Mexican horseman wearing fancy clothing
Chicano, –na (chee-cah'no, –nah) Mexican-American
chicharrones (chee-chah-ro'nays) hog cracklings; fried bits of pork
chile salsa (chee'lay sahl'sah) chili sauce
chorizo (cho-ree'so) Mexican sausage made of highly spiced pork
churro (choor'ro) type of fritter
deseo (day-say'o) desire
don (don) Sir (title of respect, used only before a man's first name)
doña (do'nyah) Lady (title given to a married woman, used only before a first name)
dulce (dool'say) sweet; gentle; mild; candy
frenesí (fray-nay-see') frenzy; madness
frijoles refritos (free-ho'lays ray-free'tos) refried beans
gallo (gah'yo) rooster; serenade (To "play the rooster" means to serenade someone.)
gringo, –ga (green'go, –gah) nickname for an English speaking person
guitarrero, –ra (gee-tar-ray'ro, –rah) guitar player or maker
hacienda (ah-see-en'dah) large ranch
¡hola! (oh'lah) hello (often used in calling to someone at a distance)
huisache (oo-ee-sah'chay) thorny bush with golden flowers

lindo, –da (leen′do, –dah) pretty
madre (mah′dray) mother
maguey (mah-gay′) agave plant used for making liquor, also for weaving and for making rope
malo, –la (mah′lo, –lah) bad; wicked; ill; difficult
manito (mah-nee′to) little brother
mano (mah′no) hand
mariachi (mah-ree-ah′chee) member of a street band
mariquita (mah-ree-kee′tah) sissy
melcocha (mel-co′chah) molasses candy
mescal (mes-cahl′) liquor made from the fermented juice of certain agave plants
mesquitales (mes-kee-tahl′ays) clumps or stands of mesquite
mesquite (mes-kee′tay) pod-bearing shrubs or small trees
mondongo (mon-don′go) tripe
morral (mor-rahl′) sack; feedbag
nombre (nom′bray) name; title
norteamericano, –na (nor′tay-ah-may-ree-cah′no, –nah) North American, most often a U.S. citizen
papacito (pah-pah-see′to) little papa
parada (pah-rah′dah) folk dance in which couples parade arm-in-arm around a room
pase (pah′say) pass
peso (pay′so) coin equal to about eight American cents
pozole (po-so′lay) spicy stew made of pork and boiled corn
pulque (pool′kay) fermented drink prepared from the maguey
ranchero (rahn-chay′ro) rancher; farm-dweller
rebozo (ray-bo′so) shawl
redil (ray-deel′) sheepfold; pen for sheep or horses
río (ree′o) river
sopa (so′pah) sometimes soup, but often a starchy dish
tequila (tay-kee′lah) alcoholic beverage made by redistilling the juices of a Mexican century plant
tequilito (tay-kee-lee′to) little bit of tequila
tío (tee′o) uncle; good old man
toro (toh′ro) bull
turista (too-rees′tah) tourist
vaquero (vah-kay′ro) cowboy; cowhand
zacate de bestia (sah-cah′tay day bes′tee-ah) hay for animals

ABCDEFGHIJ–CO–7987654321